A Closer Look at Organizational Culture in Action

Edited by Süleyman Davut Göker

Published in London, United Kingdom

IntechOpen

Supporting open minds since 2005

A Closer Look at Organizational Culture in Action
http://dx.doi.org/10.5772/intechopen.77624
Edited by Süleyman Davut Göker

Contributors
Viktor Bakhtin Viktorovich, Ashmarov Igor Anatol'yevich, Nopriadi Saputra, Ismiriati Nasip, Halvor Nordby, Md. Morshed Alom, Barbara Mazur, Süleyman Davut Göker, Mubeher Ürün Göker, Ping-Fu Hsu, Ling-Chuan Huang, Eser Erdurmazlı, Titilayo Olubunmi Olaposi

First published in London, United Kingdom, 2021 by IntechOpen
IntechOpen is the global imprint of INTECHOPEN LIMITED, registered in England and Wales, registration number: 11086078, 5 Princes Gate Court, London, SW7 2QJ, United Kingdom
Printed in Croatia

British Library Cataloguing-in-Publication Data
A catalogue record for this book is available from the British Library

Additional hard and PDF copies can be obtained from orders@intechopen.com

A Closer Look at Organizational Culture in Action
Edited by Süleyman Davut Göker
p. cm.
Print ISBN 978-1-83962-578-7
Online ISBN 978-1-83962-579-4
eBook (PDF) ISBN 978-1-83962-580-0

For EU product safety concerns:
IN TECH d.o.o., Prolaz Marije Krucifikse Kozulić 3, 51000 Rijeka, Croatia, info@intechopen.com or visit our website at intechopen.com.

Meet the editor

Süleyman Davut Göker, EdD, is currently an Associate Professor of Educational Administration and Supervision at the Faculty of Education, Canakkale 18 Mart University, Turkey. His research mainly focuses on reflective management and supervision, reflective leadership, peer coaching, reflective coaching, and curriculum development. Dr. Goker has developed an instructional supervision model in TEFL for the Ministry of Education, Turkey. Between 1999 and 2004, he worked as an Assistant Professor of TEFL and Director of the English Preparatory School, European University of Lefke, Cyprus. In 2004, he worked as a visiting scholar at the College of Education, The Ohio State University. Dr. Goker has worked in several universities in Cyprus and Turkey, such as the Eastern Mediterranean University, American University, Cyprus, Dokuz Eylul University, and Artvin Coruh University.

Contents

Preface

Culture is a driver of decisions, actions, and ultimately the overall performance of the organization; determining how employees describe where they work, how they understand the business, and how they see themselves as part of the organization. Within this context, values, beliefs, attitudes, and behaviors constitute an organization's culture and employees share and use them on a daily basis in their work. This book aims to briefly portray a new interpretation of organizational culture varying from the profusion of literature in the following ways.

It first attempts to include how cultures are created organically or through consistent planning and action in different organizations such as education, business, and health; focusing more on change and learning opportunities. It also aims to provide leaders of different organizations with experiences and reflections on how to initiate an organizational culture change as it is not an easy task. Finally, this book is expected to extend new perspectives and practices for both potential and actual managers of organizations contributing to the current debate on how to transform organizations into innovative and learning cultures.

Süleyman Davut Göker
Faculty of Education,
Çanakkale Onsekiz Mart University,
Turkey

Section 1

Dimensions of Culture in Different Organizations

Chapter 1

Public Sector Organizational Culture: Experience from Frontline Bureaucracies

Md. Morshed Alom

Abstract

This chapter discusses the practice of organizational culture by the frontline bureaucrats in Bangladesh. Culture scholars argue that organizational culture—commonly defined as the beliefs, values, attitudes, and practices of the members of an organization—is a powerful force in determining the health and well-being of an organization. Scholars also suggest the existence of different dimensions of organizational culture. Although they do not agree in naming these dimensions, commonalities are found in their understanding. How organizational culture is practiced by the frontline bureaucrats in Bangladesh has not been studied much. A study was designed to know how the frontline public bureaucrats practice organizational culture and how they differ in their practices along their service lines. Four dimensions of organizational culture—power distance, uncertainty avoidance tendency, participation, and team orientation—were considered. The chosen culture dimensions impact the overall management of any public sector organization. Three hundred and twenty-six frontline public bureaucrats were studied using a survey questionnaire. Both descriptive and inferential statistics have been used for analyzing the collected data. Findings from independent samples t-tests revealed that the frontline bureaucrats significantly differ along their service lines in practicing the culture dimensions.

Keywords: public sector, frontline bureaucracy, organizational culture

1. Introduction

Culture in public sector organizations varies in its dimensions. Organizations comprise people. People are divided into nation-states and are variably exposed to different things such as events and information, which help form their own beliefs, values, and attitudes. These differences in beliefs, values, and attitudes result in different cultural practices, which in turn get a reflection in the organizations of their respective societies. Within a society, different subgroups exist with distinct beliefs and practices. The different generational cohorts within a society become exposed to things, technologies, and events that are particular to their own time. Therefore, subgroups within a society develop thinking and behaviors that may be considered distinct. The societal general culture and subcultures affect the cultural beliefs and practices of the organizations of society.

It is generally taken for granted that culture motivates the employees of an organization to behave in a particular way. Not much research is done on how culture affects the performance of organizations. The limited number of studies investigating the cultural influence on performance reports the linkage to be positive [1, 2]. In some other contexts, despite deliberate efforts, in the public sector, organizations have shown indifference to the adoption of the prescribed culture [3]. In spite of the influences from the new public management tools, public sector organizations tend to be internal-oriented rather than being external-oriented [4]. Organizations can develop the practice of subculture, which can be considered a management technique [2, 5].

This chapter focuses on the cultural practices of the frontline bureaucrats in Bangladesh. The few studies conducted on the bureaucratic culture in Bangladesh are different from the current one in their focuses and methodologies. Jamil [6] conducted a survey in December 1992 and January 1993 on 161 bureaucrats working in both the central level administration and the field level administration and found that the bureaucrats inculcate power distance, uncertainty avoidance tendency, and are less participatory in their decision-making process. Haque and Mohammad [7], analyzing the historical accounts, relevant literature, and their observations, concluded that the prevalence of pervasive corruption in the Bangladeshi bureaucracy could be explained in terms of the existence of some culture dimensions in the public administration. Conducting 40 qualitative semi-structured interviews with bureaucrats from the central and field administration, Rahman [8] found that the bureaucrats suffer from indecision over maintaining political neutrality and political responsiveness. Zafarullah [9] found in his study of bureaucratic culture in Bangladesh that the bureaucrats support clientelism and self-preservation and oppose change initiatives. Based on personal experience and review of literature, Rashid [10] concluded that bureaucrats had less engagement with members of the civil society and non-government organizations.

The above studies had a limitation in terms of their sample size and sampling process. This study covered a larger sample chosen from the field administration only. It investigated how four dimensions of organizational culture were practiced by the frontline bureaucrats. There are two broad types of bureaucrats in the public services of the country—cadre services and non-cadre services. Recruitment, training, and mobility of the bureaucrats of these two categories are different. Therefore, how the two groups of frontline bureaucrats differ in practicing culture dimensions of power distance, uncertainty avoidance, participation, and team orientation had remained unexplored, and this has been the main objective of this study. The second section discusses how organizational culture is understood, followed by a discussion on culture dimensions in the third section. The fourth section discusses the relevance of the four dimensions of organizational culture to frontline bureaucracies, followed by a short section introducing frontline bureaucrats in Bangladesh in the fifth section. The sixth and seventh sections discuss the methods followed and the findings of the study, respectively. The last two sections present a discussion on the findings and conclusion of the study.

2. Understanding organizational culture

Hofstede, Hofstede, and Minkov [11] described culture as a "mental programming" or "software of the mind." It is shared patterns of thinking, feeling, and acting. Therefore, it is always a collective phenomenon. The patterns of thinking, feeling, and acting differentiate one group of people from others. Thus, culture is "the collective programming of the mind that distinguishes the members of one group or category of people from others" ([11] p. 6). The patterns of thinking, feeling, and acting come from the unwritten rules of the social game. The understanding of culture given by Hofstede et al. [11] is similar to that of Pettigrew ([12], p. 574), who defined it as a "system of such publicly and collectively accepted meanings operating for a given group at a given time" and provides "a general sense of orientation" to the group.

O'Reilly, Chatman, and Caldwell [13] have argued that organizational culture as a concept has a long history and goes back to early sociological studies of the early 1950s. It received prominence in the 1980s. Hofstede, Neuijen, Ohayv, and Sanders [14] found no consensus on the definition of the concept. However, they identified several characteristics of organizational culture. Organizational culture is: (1) holistic, (2) historically determined, (3) related to anthropological concepts, (4) socially constructed, (5) soft, and (6) difficult to change. Schein ([15], p. 111) published an article defining organizational culture as "(1) a pattern of basic assumptions, (2) invented, discovered, developed by a given group, (3) as it learns to cope with its problems of external adaptation and internal integration, (4) that has worked well enough to be considered valid and, therefore (5) is to be taught to new members as the (6) correct way to perceive, think, and feel in relation to these problems." Schein [15] identified three levels of organizational culture: (1) artifacts, (2) values, and (3) assumptions. However, Hofstede et al. [14], in their study, found that shared perceptions of daily practices rather than shared values represent the core of an organization's culture.

Organizational culture has also been described as an administrative culture or bureaucratic culture or corporate culture. Jamil [6] argued that there is something additional in an administrative culture than can be found in organizational culture. This additional item is politics. Most culture studies focus on the private organization where politics is not an issue of interest. These studies look at the internal context of an organization. Any framework for understanding administrative culture has to incorporate politics, i.e. how bureaucrats interact with politics and society as a whole. Jamil's [6] arguments obtain strength from the fact that the mission of public sector organizations significantly differs from that of private sector organizations. Most public sector organizations are not profit-making and do not rely on profits for their existence.

In contrast, private sector organizations are profit-oriented and rely on profits for their existence. Public sector organizations cannot avoid politics because they execute the government's policies. There is a subtle nuance between the usages of the concepts of "bureaucratic culture" and "corporate culture." The concept of bureaucratic culture refers to the values and practices in public sector organizations, while corporate culture usually refers to private sector organizations.

Whatever the characteristics or levels of organizational culture are, it is a "powerful force" in an organization [3] and immensely affects the well-being and success of an organization. It is described as the glue that holds the organization together [16]. The culture encourages the members in the organization to behave similarly. It impacts how well the organization will function. Rong and Hongwei [17] argue that organizational culture stems from the social culture and works as an "invisible hand" in public sector management. This hand is relatively stable but transforms itself in the long run in line with social change.

Lloyd [18] found that there are debates about what organizational culture is. Some believe it as what an organization "is" and others believe that it is what an organization "has." However, both arguments converge in the belief that culture is something to be made up of such concepts as beliefs, assumptions, and values. Values have received prominence in the definitions of organizational culture. Values are defined as a criterion using which one tends to prefer certain states of affairs over others. Beliefs are something that one considers as truth. The learned linkage between beliefs and values becomes attitudes. When the values, beliefs, and attitudes become so entrenched in an organization that they are no longer doubted or debated, they become assumptions. These values, beliefs, and assumptions are shared among the members of the organizations. Hofstede et al. [14] in a cross-organization study of 20 organizations in two countries found that practices rather than values play a major role. Organizational cultures are acquired on the job and are exchangeable when one takes a new job. While social cultures reside in values, organizational cultures reside in practices. These practices are visible and consciously carried out.

3. Cultural dimensions

Organizational culture is not a one-dimensional concept. Culture researchers have found different dimensions in organizational culture. Hofstede et al. [14] in their cross-organization study have identified six dimensions of organizational culture with respect to the practices where organizations differ. These dimensions are (1) process orientation vs. results orientation, (2) employee orientation vs. job orientation, (3) parochialism vs. professionalism, (4) open system vs. closed system, (5) loose control vs. tight control, and (6) normative vs. pragmatic. They argue that these dimensions may not be universally valid or sufficient. Organizational cultures in different contexts may require additional dimensions or some of the identified six dimensions may seem less useful. Along with these six practice dimensions of organizational culture, they also identified three value dimensions, which are (1) the need for security (uncertainty avoidance), (2) work centrality (job involvement), and (3) the need for authority (power distance).

The first practice dimension of organizational culture in Hofstede et al.'s [14] study opposes a concern for means to a concern for goals. They equate this contrast with the distinction made between the mechanistic and organic management systems of Burns and Stalker [19]. With a process or mechanistic orientation, an organization tends to focus on technical improvements of means rather than the accomplishment of ends. An organic system tends to focus on concern as a whole. The second practice dimension opposes concern for the employees to concern for the job to be done. In the third practice dimension, a contrast is made between the identification of the employees deriving from the organization (parochial) and the type of job (professionalism). The fourth dimension focuses on the tendency of the organization to respond to its environment. The fifth practice dimension shows the contrasts in the internal structuring of an organization. The sixth practice dimension shows how an organization is oriented toward its customers. A normative organization looks at its task toward its customers as the implementation of inviolable rules. A pragmatic organization tends to stay close to its customers. The authors distinguish results orientation from customer orientation in that "trying to serve the customer does not automatically imply a results orientation" ([14], p. 304).

Ghosh and Srivastava [20] noted that the concept of organizational culture has been interpreted differently and not all complement or converge. After reviewing a sample of the literature on the instruments used in survey studies of organizational culture, the authors concluded that no two instruments were alike, and no two instruments shared a common theoretical basis. These authors reported that Ashkanasy, Wilderom, and Peterson [21] and Wilderom, Glunk, and Maslowski [22] had studied 18 culture measure questionnaires published between 1975 and 1992 and 10 empirical culture research studies respectively. Both studies found great variation in the definition and operationalization of organizational culture and its dimensions.

Ghosh and Srivastava [20], based on Kluckhohn and Strodtbeck's [23] model, identified seven dimensions of organizational culture: (1) participation, (2) respect for individual, (3) attitude to risk, (4) attention orientation, (5) trust, (6) openness, and (7) power distance. Schein [15] in attempting to understand the content of a culture identifies some of its dimensions and presents questions to be asked regarding each dimension. Answers to these questions will identify the content of that culture, but he cautions about the danger of over-generalizing the dimensions.

Harrison and Baird [3] compared the organizational culture of public sector organizations in Australia with that of private sector organizations using O'Reilly et al.'s [13] organizational culture profile (OCP) and by focusing on five dimensions: (1) outcome orientation, (2) respect for people, (3) attention to detail, (4) team orientation, and (5) innovation. O'Reilly et al. [13] developed the OCP in order to quantitatively assess organizational culture in their study examining the person-culture fit and its implications for work attitudes and behaviors. These researchers carried out two types of factor analyses—for the individual and as organizational profiles. The first analysis produced eight dimensions of an organization's culture: (1) innovation and risk-taking, (2) attention to detail, (3) orientation toward outcome or results, (4) aggressiveness and competitiveness, (5) supportiveness, (6) emphasis on growth and rewards, (7) a collaborative and team orientation, and (8) decisiveness. The second analysis produced seven dimensions: (1) innovation, (2) stability, (3) respect for people, (4) outcome orientation, (5) attention to detail, (6) team orientation, and (7) aggressiveness. Denison and Mishra [1] used four organizational traits—involvement, adaptability, consistency, and mission—in their research to determine the relationship between organizational culture and organizational performance.

Jamil [6] studied bureaucratic culture in the context of Bangladesh in order to determine the dominant type of culture and its consequences and also to identify the bearers of administrative subcultures. He noted that most studies on organizational culture have dealt with private sector organizations. He argued that public sector organizations are different from the private sector ones in that politics play a major role in the public sector organizations. Any study about public sector organizational culture has to take into account its external context, that is, its relationship with politics and the society in general.

Jamil [6] argued that bureaucrats' attitudes in the external context could be typified in terms of their relationships to politics and relationships to citizens and civil society. In the case of the first typology, Jamil [6] argued, borrowing from Putnam [24], that bureaucrats can be classified into classical or political. Classical bureaucrats are procedure-oriented or rule-oriented, whereas political bureaucrats are problem-oriented or program-oriented. In the case of the second typology, bureaucrats can be universal or clientelistic. Universal bureaucrats believe in impartial applications of rules, which in Weberian terms are called the rational-legal type. Clientelism, on the other hand, serves in return for patronage and a power base. A recent development in the bureaucrat-citizen relationship has revealed that citizens are considered as customers in Western nations and as subjects in developing countries.

In the internal context, bureaucrats' attitudes, Jamil [6] continued, can vary in specific characteristics such as power distance, uncertainty avoidance, guiding decision-making, and preferred employees. Power distance is a character that affects the decision-making behavior of bureaucrats. Where power distance is high, top bureaucrats take decisions, and lower bureaucrats carry out them. Where power distance is low, superiors and subordinates make consultations to take decisions.

According to Jamil [6], uncertainty avoidance is another character that affects decision-making behavior as well. Bureaucrats with a high tendency toward uncertainty avoidance tend to follow the rules and regulations strictly and do not take risks. Contrarily, a low tendency toward uncertainty avoidance encourages them to take risks in terms of bending or breaking the rules.

Bureaucrats need information for making decisions. Jamil [6] argued that the nature of the decision-making structure affects information search behavior. A top-down or hierarchic type of decision-making structure leads bureaucrats to limit their information search within its boundaries, their superiors, colleagues, or juniors. However, a collegial structure of decision-making leads bureaucrats to search beyond its boundaries, that is, politicians; citizens; academic, economic, and voluntary organizations.

Another characteristic of bureaucratic decision-making, where bureaucrats differ in their attitudes, Jamil [6] argued, is preferred employees. The attribute

	Hofstede et al. [14]	Ghosh & Srivastava [20]	Harrison & Baird [3]	O'Reilly et al. [13]	Denison & Mishra [1]	Jamil [6]
1. Process vs. results orientation	√		√	√		
2. Employee vs. job orientation	√					
3. Parochialism vs. professionalism	√					
4. Open vs. closed system	√					
5. Loose vs. tight control	√					
6. Normative vs. pragmatic	√					
7. Power distance	√	√				√
8. Work centrality/Involvement/Job involvement	√				√	
9. Uncertainty avoidance/attitude to risk	√	√				√
10. Participation (external)/Adaptability/guiding decisions					√	√
11. Respect for individual/people		√	√	√		
12. Participation (internal)		√				
13. Action orientation		√				
14. Trust		√				
15. Openness		√				
16. Attention to detail			√	√		
17. Innovation			√	√		
18. Aggressiveness and competition				√		
19. Supportiveness				√		
20. Emphasis on growth and reward				√		
21. Collaborative and team orientation			√	√		
22. Stability				√		
23. Tolerance for politics						√
24. Attitude towards citizens						√
25. Attitude towards NGOs						√
26. Preferred employees						√
27. Mission					√	
28. Consistency					√	

Source: Alom ([25], p. 40).

Table 1.
Comparison of dimension of organizational culture.

of preferred employees argues that the employees for an organization should be chosen considering their social values and cultural characteristics. The social values and the cultural characteristics of the chosen employees should benefit the organization.

A comparison of the dimensions of the organizational culture identified by the different studies is presented in **Table 1**. It reveals that scholars do not agree in identifying common cultural dimensions. However, some of them agree with some of the dimensions. Some other dimensions are given different names by different authors.

4. Frontline bureaucracy and culture dimensions

Frontline bureaucracies—also known as street-level bureaucracies—are located at the bottom of the governmental pyramid. The citizens experience their government through the frontline bureaucracies because these are the service providing windows of the government. Therefore, the cultural practice of the frontline bureaucrats is of paramount importance to the government. Alom [26] identified four culture dimensions that affect transparency and accountability behaviors of the frontline bureaucrats. These culture dimensions are power distance, uncertainty avoidance tendency, participation, and team orientation. One of the critical features of good governance is accountability, which comes through transparency. In this sense, the four culture dimensions affect good governance the most.

Most frontline bureaucracies bear two common characteristics—they enjoy discretion but suffer from resources. The resource limitation characteristic may vary from context to context based on economic development of the countries, but discretion has been reported to exist irrespective of the level of economic development. Discretion is a structural feature, while resources are issues of an endowment. Therefore, these are not cultural factors. However, these factors in interaction with the cultural beliefs and practices—power distance, uncertainty avoidance, participation, and team orientation—may impact on the good governance practices of the frontline bureaucrats. A brief discussion of these four cultural beliefs and practices is given below.

Power Distance: Power distance is the tendency to accept inequality among ranks in the system [14]. Bureaucrats, in socially backward contexts such as Bangladesh, believe that they are socially superior, and they are not accountable to the service seekers. They protect this power position. Therefore, any reform initiatives that are directed to change this power position are not acceptable to them or at least will hinder the implementation of such initiatives [27, 28]. Redistribution of power in a social structure that has traditionally practiced a patron-client relationship among its members is particularly problematic. Bureaucrats that possess power distance in relation to their clients will also possess the same in their organizational structure. Rong and Hongwei [17] suggested that organizational culture stems from social cultures. Jamil's [6] study supports this argument. He found that the traditions from the samaj (society as a whole) and the British colonial administration dominate bureaucratic culture in Bangladesh. The samaj and the colonial traditions maintain a hierarchical or patron-client social structure. The influence of these traditions is reflected in the bureaucracy in the form of high power distance. Therefore, high power distance supports a hierarchical power structure in the organization as well as in society.

Uncertainty Avoidance: Bureaucrats do not want to be in uncomfortable situations. In other words, they like to avoid situations or avoid anything that may create situations, putting them in trouble or discomfort. They want to be certain that any action committed by them will not bring them discomfort. According to Zafarullah ([9], p. 936), "The civil service in Bangladesh has shown an extraordinary predilection to hang on to the established rather than readily accepting change in its status, structure, functions, and norms of engagement with extra-bureaucratic instruments." The bureaucrats are "more at ease operating in a familiar environment employing conventional practices than embracing anything new or different" ([9], p. 936).

Participation: Participation is allowing those in the decision-making process for whom decisions are being made. In other words, it refers to the quality, quantity, and diversity of input from the stakeholders in government decisions [29]. Organizations that are under stronger influence from external stakeholders are likely to exhibit a higher level of participation. In Jamil's [6] language, this type of participation is guiding decisions, that is, how the decisions of the bureaucrats are guided. Do the frontline bureaucrats consult with their stakeholders, that is, politicians; citizens; and business and voluntary organizations? A bureaucrat's attitude toward the level of interaction with its stakeholders regarding the decision-making process influences the practice of participation.

Team Orientation: Practice of teamwork increases productivity in organizations. A team is a group of individuals who share their responsibilities to accomplish their shared goals [30]. Group members have discretion in deciding how to carry out tasks and allocate tasks among themselves [31]. Team orientation is a dimension of organizational culture identified by Schein [15] and O'Reilly et al. [13] and has been used by Harrison and Baird [3] in their research. Hierarchical structures in public bureaucracies work as barriers to team building. A public sector organization is a "machine bureaucracy" that needs to change its hierarchically controlled managerial culture into "a coaching environment" where the individuals will appreciate "interpersonal needs and the benefits of intuition and creativity" (Lovell [32], p. 403).

5. Frontline bureaucrats in Bangladesh

The frontline public bureaucracy in Bangladesh represents the characteristics of the overall public service of the country. These characteristics descended from the British colonial administration and the post-colonial administration of Pakistan. Bangladesh was liberated from Pakistan through a liberation war in 1971. Considering the recruitment, training, and mobility of the bureaucrats, one characteristic of the public services in Bangladesh has been that they are divided into cadre and non-cadre services. The cadre services have distinct hierarchy and specified functions—specialized and generalized [33]. The members of these services belong to the Bangladesh Civil Service (BCS) who are recruited by the Public Service Commission (PSC) through highly competitive examinations. They are hired as Assistant Secretary or equivalent and can move to the Senior Secretary position through promotions. They can move from one department to another. On the other hand, members of the non-cadre services are recruited to particular departments and do not have a definite structure of mobility horizontally and vertically [34]. They need to serve within the department to which they are recruited. These bureaucrats have limited training opportunity throughout their service life. The frontline bureaucracy of Bangladesh has officials from both cadre and non-cadre services, but the size of the former category is smaller than the later.

6. Methods

Data for this study were collected from sub-district level frontline bureaucrats in Bangladesh using a survey questionnaire. Bangladesh had 488 sub-districts at the time of data collection. Twenty-nine sub-districts were chosen using a multistage sampling technique. From each of the selected sub-districts, 16 pre-decided office heads out of around 25 were given the questionnaire to fill out. The 16 office heads were chosen because they were perceived by practitioners as the frontline bureaucracies that had most interactions with citizens. Seven of these 16 offices are headed by cadre officials, and the rest nine offices are headed by non-cadre officials.

For data collection, the researcher traveled to the respondents. It was not possible to return with all filled-out questionnaires all the time. Therefore, questionnaires were left with the offices of those respondents where they were not available in their offices. It was not possible to contact each of these office heads before going to their offices. Instead, the chief executive officer (UNO) of the sub-district was contacted before going to that particular sub-district. The UNO office in a sub-district carries some importance because it plays a coordinating role among all the offices of the sub-district. After going to a sub-district, help from officials from the UNO office was obtained sometimes in distributing and collecting the questionnaires. Thus, the UNO office was used as the first contact point.

After going to a sub-district, this researcher went to each of the 16 selected offices in the sub-district. Where the office head was present, this researcher requested him or her to fill out the survey questionnaire. Where the office head was not present, his/her contact cell phone number was collected from the other officials of the office. Then the office head was contacted over the phone and requested to fill out the survey questionnaire when he/she was available in the office and was requested either to send the filled out questionnaire to the UNO office or the postal address of this researcher. In most cases, an envelope (with postage stamp) was left with the postal address of the researcher written on it.

Around 40% of the survey questionnaires, on average, were collected directly by the researcher. Some filled out questionnaires came directly from the respondents through the postal service. The remaining questionnaires were submitted to the UNO office, or the officials of the UNO office collected them from the other offices and then sent them together to the researcher through postal service. Altogether, 329 questionnaires were collected for the study out of the sample of 456. This constituted a response rate of 72.15%. However, three questionnaires were rejected because two of them had more than 50% items unanswered, and one was a duplicate. The duplication happened because one officer was in charge of two offices. That official filled out two questionnaires. Thus, one of these two questionnaires was rejected. Finally, data from 326 questionnaires were entered into the SPSS program. Demographic information of the respondents is presented in **Table 2**.

The questionnaire had items taken from validated instruments to measure each of the cultural dimensions. Each item had a four-point scale which varied from "always" to "never" or "agree" to "disagree." A five-item scale was constructed based on Jamil [6] to measure power distance. The items were: (1) I seek my subordinates' opinions before making a decision; (2) My subordinates suggest me ideas about my office work; (3) Confident subordinates in my office disagree with my decisions; (4) I tell my subordinates what decisions are to be taken; and (5) When I am confident, I disagree with my higher authority. To measure uncertainty avoidance, a four-item scale was developed based on Jamil [6] which were: (1) I emphasize results more than following routines, procedures to the point; (2) I feel nervous about satisfying my higher authority with my work; (3) I look for the best alternative even if it

(1) Sex:		(3) Education		(5) Nature of service	
Male	291(89)	Bachelor	105(32)	Cadre	144(44)
Female	35(11)	Master	209(67)	Non-cadre	182(56)
		PhD	2(1)		
(2) Age		(4) Career (years in service):			
26-35	79(25)	1-5	147(46)		
36-45	108(37)	6-10	87(27)		
46-55	97(30)	11-15	30(9)		
56-	29(9)	16-20	30(9)		
		≥21	25(8)		

Table 2.
Demographic information of respondent (% in parenthesis).

goes beyond routines, and procedures; (4) I expect my higher authority to tell me if I am doing a good job. Participation was measured using a four-item scale developed following theoretical arguments. The items were: (1) My office should serve citizens according to their preferences; (2) Officers can learn nothing from service seekers; (3) My office should seek feedback from service recipients about their satisfaction; and (4) Service seekers should not advise us on what to do. Based on Harrison and Baird [3], a four-item scale was used to measure team orientation. The items were: (1) Working in teams can produce better results; (2) We should help each other in our office work; (3) Sometimes subordinates can give better opinions than superiors; (4) Subordinates should not disagree with the superior's opinion.

7. Findings

Results of two independent samples t-tests and descriptive statistics of group differences in the means of the culture dimensions practiced by the cadre and non-cadre officials are presented in **Table 3**. Power distance in non-cadre officials is higher than in cadre officials. The difference is significant at 0.10 level of significance. Concerning uncertainty avoidance, the non-cadre officials again have a significantly higher tendency to avoid uncertainty compared to the cadre officials. The cadre officials' mean score in the participation culture dimension is significantly higher than the mean score of the non-cadre officials. This finding is indicative of the cadre officials' higher tendency to accommodate stakeholders in decision-making processes. With regard to team orientation, the mean score of cadre officials

Culture Dimension	Group						95% CI for Mean Difference	t	df	Sig.
	Cadre			Non-Cadre						
	M	SD	n	M	SD	n				
Power Distance	2.20	.40	145	2.28	.43	179	-0.17, 0.02	-1.64	319	.10
Uncertainty Avoidance	2.54	.52	143	2.70	.51	182	-0.27, -0.05	-2.79	323	.01
Participation	3.47	.55	141	3.34	.53	181	0.01, 0.25	2.17	320	.03
Team Orientation	3.46	.32	144	3.39	.31	182	-0.00, 0.14	1.93	324	.05

Table 3.
Results of t-test and descriptive statistics for culture dimensions by cadre.

is also significantly higher than the non-cadre officials. Therefore, cadre officials possess a higher mentality of teamwork compared to non-cadre officials.

8. Discussion

The four culture dimensions influence the daily works of the frontline bureaucrats. Generally, power distance within an office context is an extension of the power distance that prevails in society. High power distance among the employees of an organization contributes to the fortification of its formal and rigid hierarchical structure. The cadre officials of the frontline bureaucracies inculcate this culture slightly less than the non-cadre officials and both scores are slightly lower than the average of the scale. Jamil [6] reported the existence of higher power distance in the cadre officials in general (central and frontline bureaucrats). Power distance in this study shows scores lower than the average (2.5 points on the scale of 4). Therefore, this culture has not changed much.

The culture of uncertainty avoidance tendency negatively affects the achievement of the targeted results of an organization. It bars officials from taking initiatives of innovation. Strict enforcement of bureaucratic procedures, in some contexts, may not fetch the desired results. Therefore, officials need to apply their discretion and take some risks, which might bring them some uncertainty. Generally, everyone wants to remain in his comfort zone. In public service delivery, when facing the complexity of local contexts, frontline bureaucrats need to come out of their comfort zones sometimes. This study found high uncertainty tendency in the frontline bureaucrats. The non-cadre officials have a greater tendency to avoid uncertainty than the cadre officials. High level of uncertainty avoidance tendency among the bureaucrats in Bangladesh was reported by Jamil [6], and the current scenario does not show any change.

Participation in this research was used to mean bureaucrats' citizen-orientation, that is, their attitude toward feedback from citizens. The frontline bureaucrats directly deliver services to the citizens. Their understanding of the expectations of the citizens can equip them with appropriate services. The findings of this study show that the frontline bureaucrats have a very high tendency to get feedback from the citizens. Again the cadre officials are ahead of the non-cadre ones. This finding is also similar to that of Jamil [6].

The frontline bureaucrats show a positive attitude toward teamwork. The score of cadre officials is higher than the non-cadre officials. These frontline bureaucrats work in their offices with limited resources. They face huge workloads as well. These workloads happen because of two reasons. One reason is that the demand for services is very high. Bangladesh is a populous country. So these bureaucrats face more service seekers than the ideal size. The second reason is that many of the sanctioned positions in the frontline bureaucracies remain vacant. Therefore, the bureaucrats from within an organization need to cooperate among themselves through teamwork.

9. Conclusion

Organizational culture is difficult to change without a deliberate effort. In the public sector organizations, this change is even harder to bring. The bureaucrats are rule followers and change-resistant. They remain to be in their comfort zones. Bringing desired changes in the practice of culture will require conscious and deliberate efforts. These efforts may include education, training, and social campaign. The difference in the scores in the dimensions of culture practiced by the cadre and non-cadre bureaucrats can be attributed to the different outlook they develop through their participation in social events. Although both groups of bureaucrats come from the same social context, they become exposed to different social events. One obvious social event is training. The cadre bureaucrats take part in different long- and short-term training programs even at the very beginning of their services. The non-cadre bureaucrats hardly get any training. The second social factor is that the cadre bureaucrats, because of their mobility, attend various seminars and workshops on governance issues, which help them change their mindset. This scope is limited to the non-cadre bureaucrats.

This research had limitations. The items used to measure the culture dimensions in this research match the research context. The measurement tools might be different in other contexts. Future researchers can investigate why the cadre and non-cadre officials differ significantly in their organizational culture.

Author details

Md. Morshed Alom
Bangladesh Public Administration Training Centre, Dhaka, Bangladesh

*Address all correspondence to: mmapatc@hotmail.com

References

[1] Denison DR, Mishra AK. Toward a theory of organizational culture and effectiveness. Organization Science. 1995;**6**(2):204-223

[2] Shin Y, Kim M, Choi JN, Lee SH. Does team culture matter? Roles of team culture and collective regulatory focus in team task and creative performance. Group & Organization Management. 2016;**41**(2):232-265

[3] Harrison GL, Baird KM. The organizational culture of public sector organizations in Australia. Australian Journal of Management. 2015;**40**(4):613-629

[4] Bradley L, Parker R. Do Australian public sector employees have the type of culture they want in the era of new public management? Australian Journal of Public Administration. 2006;**65**(1):89-99

[5] Sinclair A. Public sector culture managerialism or multiculturalism? Australian Journal of Public Administration. 1989;**48**(4):382-397

[6] Jamil I. Administrative culture in Bangladesh: Tensions between tradition and modernity. International Review of Sociology/Revue Internationale de Sociologie. 2002;**12**(1):93-125

[7] Haque ST, Mohammad SN. Administrative culture and incidence of corruption in Bangladesh: A search for the potential linkage. International Journal of Public Administration. 2013;**36**(13):996-1006

[8] Rahman MS. Bureaucratic perceptions to the politics–bureaucracy relations in Bangladesh: A moral dilemma in between political neutrality and responsiveness. Asian Journal of Political Science. 2014;**22**(3):252-267

[9] Zafarullah H. Bureaucratic culture and the social-political connection: The Bangladesh example. International Journal of Public Administration. 2013;**36**(13):932-939

[10] Rashid AK. The role of the bureaucracy in policymaking in Bangladesh. Asia Pacific Journal of Public Administration. 2014;**36**(2):150-161

[11] Hoftede G, Hofstede GJ, Minkov M. Cultures and Organizations: Software of the Mind: Intercultural Cooperation and its Importance for Survival. New York: McGraw-Hill; 2010

[12] Pettigrew AM. On studying organizational cultures. Administrative Science Quarterly. 1979;**24**(4):570-581

[13] O'Reilly CA III, Chatman J, Caldwell DF. People and organizational culture: A profile comparison approach to assessing person-organization fit. Academy of Management Journal. 1991;**34**(3):487-516

[14] Hofstede G, Neuijen B, Ohayv DD, Sanders G. Measuring organizational cultures: A qualitative and quantitative study across twenty cases. Administrative Science Quarterly. 1990;**1**:286-316

[15] Schein EH. Organizational culture. The American Psychologist. 1990;**45**(2):109-119

[16] Banerjee P. A study of effective team building in relation to organizational culture and organizational climate in universities in Delhi. Higher Education for the Future. 2014;**1**(2):211-225

[17] Tan R, Sun H. Transformations of organizational culture in the public sector. Cross-Cultural Communication. 2012;**8**(4):46-52

[18] Lloyd E. Organizational culture. In: Raisa A M, Stephen P, editors.

Organizational Behavior. London: Kogan Page Ltd; 2013. p. 209-240

[19] Burns T, Stalker GM. The Management of Innovation. London: Tavistock; 1961

[20] Ghosh S, Srivastava BK. Construction of a reliable and valid scale for measuring organizational culture. Global Business Review. 2014;**15**(3):583-596

[21] Ashkanasy NM, Wilderom CP, Peterson MF. Handbook of Organizational Culture and Climate. Thousands Oak, CA: Sage; 2000

[22] Wilderom CP, Glunk U, Maslowski R. Handbook of Organizational Culture and Climate. Thousands Oak, CA: Sage; 2000

[23] Kluckhohn FR, Strodtbeck FL. Variations in Value Orientations. Evanston, IL: Row, Peterson; 1961

[24] Putnam RD. The political attitudes of senior civil servants in Britain, Germany, and Italy. In: Dogan M, editor. The Mandarins of Western Europe: The Political Role of Top Civil Servants. Vol. 1975. New York: John Wiley; 1975. pp. 87-128

[25] Alom MM. Proactive transparency and outward accountability in the public sector: The perspective of the frontline public bureaucrats in Bangladesh. Doctoral Dissertation. Bangkok, Thailand: National Institute of Development Administration; 2016

[26] Alom MM. Proactive transparency and outward accountability of frontline public bureaucracies: An integrated model. International Journal of Productivity and Performance Management. 2018;**67**(4):611-628

[27] Flinders M. The politics of accountability: A case study of freedom of information legislation in the United Kingdom. The Political Quarterly. 2000;**71**(4):422-435

[28] Grimmelikhuijsen S, Porumbescu G, Hong B, Im T. The effect of transparency on trust in government: A cross-national comparative experiment. Public Administration Review. 2013;**73**(4):575-586

[29] Welch EW. The relationship between transparent and participative government: A study of local governments in the United States. International Review of Administrative Sciences. 2012;**78**(1):93-115

[30] Cohen SG, Bailey DE. What makes teams work: Group effectiveness research from the shop floor to the executive suite. Journal of Management. 1997;**23**(3):239-290

[31] Langfred CW. Too much of a good thing? Negative effects of high trust and individual autonomy in self-managing teams. Academy of Management Journal. 2004;**47**(3):385-399

[32] Lovell R. Citizen's charter: The cultural challenge. Public Administration. 1992;**70**(3):395-404

[33] Siddiquee NA, Faroqi MG. Equal employment opportunity in the public service: Theory and practice in Bangladesh. International Journal of Public Administration. 2010;**33**(8-9):451-462

[34] Ahmed SG. Composition and structure of Services in Bangladesh. Indian Journal of Public Administration. 1984;**30**(1):184-210

Chapter 2

Organizational Culture under Religious Influence

Barbara Mazur

Abstract

Based on a review of articles and other published research work as well as the results of the author's research conducted in organizations operating in religiously diverse environments in Poland, this chapter examines the influence of religion on organizational culture. The most important findings of this work concern the vital role religion plays in an organization and its culture. This paper examines religion's influence on organizational culture, which is considered as an independent variable. It proposes a model of organizational culture enriched by the channel by which religion enters the organization's set of values and norms. The chapter consists of the following parts: the analysis of the role of religion in an organization in the light of hitherto research, cultural dimensions of religion, analytical approaches to organizational culture, the integrated model of organizational culture enhanced by the aspect of religion, and the research results confirming the influence of Catholic and Orthodox religions on organizational culture.

Keywords: Catholic and Orthodox religion, dimensions of national culture, basic assumptions, organizational culture

1. Introduction

Organizational culture is an important element in the functioning of an enterprise, which is why it is worth considering the problem of its formation and especially its conditions. Organizational culture is influenced by many factors, ranging from the type of organization, through its characteristics and the characteristics of its participants, to the type of environment it operates in. Researchers of organizational culture determinants attach great importance to the national aspect, indicating that the manifestations of national culture appear both in the category related to the environment and in the characteristics of participants, which proves the role of national culture in shaping organizational culture [1]. External research determinants of organizational culture have been clearly less important in religion. Its impact on organizational culture was not as often analyzed by management theorists as the impact of national culture. However, it must be acknowledged that religion is a source of values and norms and in this sense has a culture-forming nature, becoming one of the pillars of organizational culture [1]. The issue of the impact of religion on organizations and their cultures is becoming increasingly important in the context of globalization and economic integration.

2. The role of religion in an organization

National culture and religion are interrelated because the shape of national culture is influenced by adopted and professed religion. According to Hofstede [2], the type and version of the religion adopted in a given country is the result of previously existing cultural patterns in a given area and a culture-forming factor. He writes that religion adopted in a given country strengthens existing cultural models, making them basic elements of its doctrine [2].

The religious factor is not only a determinant of cultural norms, values, and rules of individual and community conduct, but also has significant formative influence in the field of business. The issues of the cultural dimension of religion and its impact on the problem of work were raised by researchers such as Max Weber and Peter Berger, whose works belong to the most important traditions in social sciences. They pointed to important relations between religion, work, and economy.

Sources of values in organizational culture are therefore cultural qualities existing in the environment of organizations. Those include the region's culture, national culture, religious culture, and personal characteristics of the members of the organization, which—to a large extent—are shaped by the cultural environment of the individual [3]. Religion, being a part of the cultural environment of the organization, affects organizational culture in particular through two of the four factors determining it: the personal characteristics of the organization's participants and the type of environment in which the organization operates [4]. Under homogeneous conditions, they remain similar, while under heterogeneity conditions, they may differ. Religious norms in business act as archetypes: they are passed on in the circles of followers of individual religions from generation to generation and as a result penetrate the collective consciousness, becoming its hidden element conditioning the shape of economic life. As a result, religion plays an important role in the workplace.

The impact of religion on the work process cannot be overestimated because work and religion and their relationships are fundamental components, building blocks of human society [5]. Research to date, although largely fragmentary, has confirmed the existence of a relationship between religion and attitudes toward work. It has also shown the religion's connection to motivation, job satisfaction, and even the degree of commitment to work. In social life, the role of religion is that it equips its followers with a system of values to which they should live. This system, however, also applies to the work environment. Many business practitioners accept the assertion of the need to understand the role of religion as imperative, being convinced that it strongly influences organizational life [6]. Research also shows that employees often turn to God when forced to make difficult decisions. The role of religion is appreciated not only by practitioners but also by management theorists, who, like Trompenaars and Woolliams [7], recognize it as the second most important, after nationality, variable in the cultural dimension of individualism. Since referring only to nationality turns out to be insufficient to explain all the differences between employees in an international organization, it is worth reaching for the denominational cultural values of employees.

3. The cultural dimension of religion

The issue of the cultural dimension of religion indicates the internal dichotomy of religion, which on the one hand includes beliefs and related behaviors regarding what is supernatural and oriented to eternal salvation, on the other—constitutes a specific type of culture. To emphasize the culture-forming role of religion, Geertz [8] uses the term cultural dimension of religion-culture being understood as embodied in symbols, as a pattern of meanings passed down from generation to generation, a system of inherited images expressed in symbolic forms through which people convey, consolidate, and develop their knowledge of life and attitude toward it. The role of religion in the social and economic life of human communities is not undermined, and among the representatives of the world of science, religion is widely recognized as an important social institution.

Throughout the literature in the field of management, the concept of spirituality is often combined with religion. This position is represented by Benner [9], for whom spirituality means the process of establishing and maintaining a relationship with God. And although not all scholars consider separating spirituality from religiosity, they consider the difference between spirituality and religiosity as largely artificial. They often understand spirituality as values recognized by people and meanings that sometimes embody religious beliefs.

Spirituality, like religion, carries strict cultural connotations. Mitroff and Denton [10] argue that spirituality is a vital human need that should be recognized as fundamental to human experience and should, therefore, be a part of organizational culture. These researchers proposed a new paradigm in the study of organizations. It incorporates concepts such as supernatural forces, showing businesses the path to spirituality-based organizations.

4. Levels of cultural programming

Culture, as Hofstede defines it, is a collective mind programming that distinguishes members of one group from another. People were equipped with "mental programs," which in early childhood are developed in the family circle and then strengthened during education and work. Three levels of programming can be distinguished: universal (objective), cultural (intersubjective), and individual (subjective) [11].

Listed as the first, the universal level covers the biological functions of the human body, but also expressive behaviors such as laughter and crying, as well as associative and expressive behaviors existing in higher mammals.

Mental programming on a cultural, intersubjective level is almost entirely learned. This level is analogous for all those who, although they are not carriers of the same genes, are subjected to the same socialization process and identify with the same culture. The individual programming level is characteristic for each person, which means that there are no two identically programmed people. This level includes individual personality, although subjective to some extent, it is partly genetically determined.

Everyone's mental programming process is in part unique, in part the same as in other people [12]. Nevertheless, it can be said that people within a given culture think, feel, and react in a certain way which is why they gain in a sense a collective personality.

5. Organizational culture research approaches

The issues of organizational culture are widely recognized as extremely important in the context of organizational management. From many existing definitions of organizational culture, one should be chosen that combines and integrates various cultural concepts. The perception of organizational culture should be divided into three perspectives: an independent (external) variable, a dependent (internal) variable, and a core metaphor.

Recognizing culture as an independent variable is important for studying the relationship between culture and elements of the management process. In this approach, culture is an explanatory factor or a broad frame of reference that affects specific elements of the management process. Culture from the outside influences the employee and the managerial behavior in a given country and directly determines it. From this perspective, one can compare management and employee attitudes in different countries. The cultural values of a given country influence what is happening in organizations operating in its area. In comparative studies on management methods, the culture of a given country is considered the basic tool of analysis. It answers the question concerning the reasons for behavior in the workplace. This approach included research on national management styles and comparative research on the impact of cultural context on organizations. Culture is understood in functionalist categories and serves as a context affecting the management process. Organizational culture is interpreted as a product of the impact of a given country's culture [4].

Organizational culture is also treated as an element of the organization which depends on the existence of other organizational elements, for example, ownership and transaction costs, activities of the entrepreneur or organizational leaders. This is a dependent variable. In this approach, one can speak of organizational culture management. In this context, leadership is attributed to management. Culture as an internal variable is part of the overarching whole. It is perceived from the point of view of the function it performs for the organization and the way this function is performed.

Employers use a cultural form of regulating behavior as it is cheaper than a bureaucratic or market form. An investment is made in intensive employee training, during which they undergo specific educational, indoctrinating procedures that shape their new values, behavior norms, and daily habits. According to critics of this approach, the importance of the impact of a given country's culture on the functioning of an organization is being diminished. Besides, organizational culture is a "black box" in which it is not known exactly what is going on, but only what is affecting it from the outside. The significance of work and formal organizations for individuals can only be inferred from the description of behavior and indicators obtained from surveys [13].

Organizational culture can also be understood as a native metaphor. It is perceived as an indeterministic model of analysis in which culture is treated as an autonomous entity, not determined by the culture occurring in the environment of a given country, or by other factors of the internal environment of the organization. Culture is treated as a form of expression or manifestation of human consciousness. Research in this approach focuses on the exploration of the phenomenon of an organization as a matter of subjective experience and analyzes patterns that make "organized activities possible." These patterns include rules of action inscribed in the basic assumptions, language, knowledge, and symbols such as myths, ideologies, rituals, and organizational stories. In this perspective, qualitative methods are usually used in research – field research and case studies [14].

Organizations are shaped in the course of everyday interactions. They objectify themselves through joint actions of individuals. The following interactive processes occurring in the organization can be observed: struggle, games, manipulations or negotiations. They give the final character to the company, assuming that they constantly change it. The organization has a processual character. The "black box" of organizational culture is opened and subjected to description and analysis. This is an approach that departs from functionalism but allows understanding of what is happening in the organization. It explains phenomena such as conflicts, threats, and resistance to change. Critics of this concept accuse it of "being focused mainly on the description of organizational culture, and not on explaining it; on concepts specific to given cultures, and not on universal concepts. Therefore, it is difficult to use general statements explaining the reasons for the occurrence of certain phenomena in the organization" [14].

By considering organizational culture with three different perspectives at the same time, one can get an integrated analysis model, which is a synergistic effect of these interpretations. "Such a definition of the organizational culture, which includes values and norms, systems shared in a given organization, and derived from its environment, colloquial and often unconscious assumptions and related to them, produced by members of the organization, rules of operation, go beyond the limitations of the model treating organizational culture as an independent variable and as a dependent variable, as well as beyond the indeterministic model of analyzing this phenomenon" [4].

The combination of three epistemological perspectives allows a better understanding of the complex phenomenon of organizational culture. In the integrated model, organizational culture is determined by the national culture of a given country, it also depends on the internal elements of the organization, as well as being partly independent of these fields, due to the autonomy of human activities in the organization. Religion influences the shape of organizational culture in each of the three approaches presented. For the purposes of this article, to show this impact, organizational culture will be analyzed on the assumption that it is an independent variable conditioned by existing religion.

6. Religion, social environment, and organizational culture

Recognizing culture as an independent variable is important for studying the relationship between ambient culture and elements of the management process. In this approach, culture is an explanatory factor or a broad frame of reference that affects specific elements of the management process. The culture of the external environment of organization influences employee and managerial behavior in a given country and directly determines it. From this perspective, you can compare management and employee attitudes in different countries. The culture values of a given country influence what is happening in organizations. In comparative studies on management methods, the culture of the country is considered the basic tool of analysis. It answers the question about the reasons for behavior in the workplace.

The culture of the social environment, being the external environment of the organization, affects the culture of the organization. It is therefore reasonable and necessary to subject it to a more detailed analysis. National culture is the most frequently indicated factor determining the value of organizational culture. Hofstede indicates that the dimensions of national culture are positively correlated with some characteristic of organizational culture [12]. They also prove that combining organizational culture with national culture results in high job satisfaction, improves decision-making processes, and is positively correlated with the effectiveness of activities in the organization [4]. National culture, being part of the cultural environment of the organization, affects organizational culture through all of the factors mentioned.

Therefore, since the category of enterprise culture is a product of the socio-cultural and economic context in which the enterprise operates [4], norms, attitudes, and values are transferred to the enterprise to a large extent from its external environment. It is assumed that there is a diffusion of values and norms from the culture of society to organizational culture [15].

Social culture cannot be narrowed down to the sphere of values, as it also includes the sphere of moral practices recognized in society. Therefore, the impact of social culture on organizational culture occurs not only through values but also the practices that result from them.

Although one of the important factors influencing the organizational culture is the national culture of the country in which the organization operates, the dimensions of the national culture do not translate directly – mechanically into the organizational culture of companies [16].

It can be assumed that since specific values occur at the level of a given society, they should also be visible at the organizational and individual levels.

From three levels of cultural programming, religion shapes organizational cultures by programming on two levels: almost entirely learned cultural level and partly, to some extent genetically determined, individual. Programming at the cultural level reflects the basic cultural assumptions, while programming at the individual level—the values of organizational culture. Culture is a collection of religious values that are, at least partly, individual for people living in the same social environment [17].

7. Organizational culture: structure, terms, and components

Schein [18, 19] created a structural model of culture, which is used as a framework in analyzing organizational culture in this study. The reason to use this particular model is two-fold: it has received less criticism than other models [20] and it has been operationalized before [21, 22]. Therefore, this research assumes a particular understanding of *organizational culture.* It is a pattern of shared basic assumptions, which have been created, discovered, or developed by a given group while it learned to cope with its problems of external adaptation and internal integration. This pattern of basic assumptions has proved its usefulness in the past, and therefore is validated to be transferred to the new group members. It will serve as the correct way to perceive, comprehend, and act on those problem areas [18].

Schein [18, 19] maintains that examining culture should be based on examining the deeply held basic assumptions in a group as those historical structures tend to be kept by the members in an almost unconscious realm. They fulfill their objectives directing, guiding, and giving meaning to one's relations with nature, reality, and others. Those values and shared basic assumptions are believed to materialize themselves in the form of artifacts. Given a number of layered levels of culture, Schein [18, 19] proposes that a structure of organizational culture is best represented by a multi-level figure as presented below, in **Figure 1**.

Organizational culture encompasses a cognitive component, which consists of mutual assumptions, beliefs, norms, and attitudes that the organization's members share, and which also shape their mental (interpretative) schemes [23–25]. Therefore, organizational culture shapes and determines the way members perceive, construe, and behave in their immediate surroundings. The cognitive component of organizational culture is responsible for the way that unique meaning and reaction are ascribed to phenomena within and outside the organization.

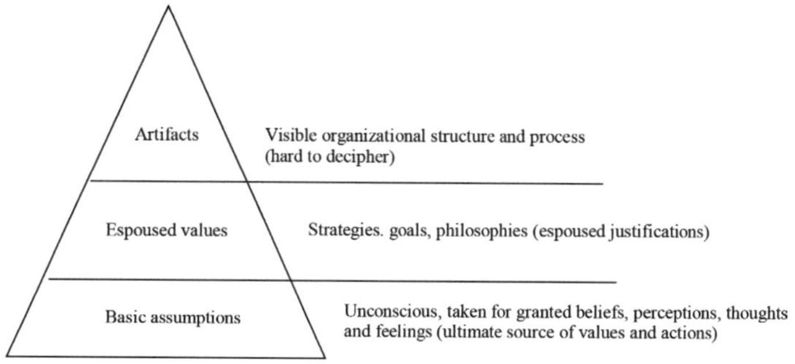

Figure 1.
Structural model of organizational culture indicating different levels of culture. Source: [19], p. 17.

While imposing a set of assumptions and values, organizational culture defines its members' perceptions, interpretations, and actions [26].

Inevitably, organizational culture impacts therefore all the processes taking place in an organization, as well as, eventually, its performance. Through organization's members' mental maps, culture can influence organization's: leadership style, learning, knowledge management, business strategy, the preferred style of changing management, employee reward system, or employee commitment.

This study is carried out at the level of the organization and is premised upon the fact that there appear similar patterns of culture across organizations operating in a particular region. This region can be understood as either defined by geography or general societal culture. However, it must be underlined that organizational culture is also dependent on factors external to the organization. Furthermore, some differences between organizational cultures in organizations can be explained by similar variations in culture-producing forces external to those organizations on the societal level [20]. Consequently, organizations should not be conceptualized as "cultural islands" or a "mini-societies." Instead, it seems to be useful to define organizational culture as a nexus where broader, societal dimensions of culture converge [27].

8. The operationalization of basic assumptions of organizational culture

This study is conditioned on the basis that value dimensions can serve to differentiate one culture from another. Therefore, value dimensions are applied to help illustrate the expected differences occurring between the researched organizations.

The most commonly adopted framework for culture research is the one developed by Hofstede. It was created for the first large-scale study of culture. Moreover, it has been praised by reviewers for its rigorous research design, a systematic data collection, and a coherent theory to explain national variations [28].

Through empirical research, Hofstede has identified four main dimensions which distinguish between cultures. In the business context, those four values have been repeatedly found relevant as well, especially when analyzing and clarifying differences observed in leadership styles [29] or managerial skills [30]. The four dimensions are considered to be suitable and fitting when examining differences in basic underlying assumptions of organizational cultures [4, 16].

Hofstede's dimensions represent *what* issues all societies had in common. Those matters include the power in relationships, the ambiguity of life, the influences of groups, and the nurturing perspectives. Each of the dimensions is presented with its basic assumptions [31, 32] as in the tables below (**Tables 1–4**).

- *Individualism* refers to the identity of self as based either solely on the individual or on the individual as part of a group or collective.
- *Power distance* refers to the social stratification within a society in which higher status individuals/groups are ascribed more power and authority by those of lower status.
- *Uncertainty avoidance* refers to the society's fear of the unknown or ambiguous situations.
- *Masculinity* (assertiveness) refers to a society's preference for competition and outcomes (masculine values) as opposed to co-operation and process (feminine values).

A model of basic underlying assumptions of organizational culture, which is determined by societal/national culture and through it by religion, has been created. The model is presented in **Figure 2** below.

This comprehensive model, embracing basic underlying assumptions of culture, can be used to describe organizational culture.

Individualism	Collectivism
People are independent	People are interdependent
One's identity draws from individual personality	One's identity draws from belonging to a group
People are not emotionally dependent on organizations or groups	People need to be emotionally dependent on organizations or groups
Individual achievement is ideal	Group achievement is ideal
The individual protects him/herself and his/her relatives	The group protects its members in exchange for their loyalty
Making decisions individually is best	Making decisions as a group is best
Source: [33], p. 119.	

Table 1.
General assumptions in individualism *vs.* collectivism.

Small power distance	High power distance
Inequality is fundamentally bad	Inequality is fundamentally good
Everyone plays a different role	Everyone has a place; some are high, and some are low in social structure
People are interdependent	Most people should be dependent on the leader
All people should have the same rights	The powerful are entitled to privileges
The powerful should hide their power	The powerful should demonstrate their power
Source: [33], p. 120.	

Table 2.
General assumptions in power distance.

Small uncertainty avoidance	High uncertainty avoidance
Conflict should not be avoided	Conflict should be avoided at any cost
Deviant people and ideas should be tolerated	Deviant people and ideas should not be tolerated
Laws are not very important and should not be followed	Laws are very important and should be followed
Experts and authorities are not usually correct	Experts and authorities are usually correct
Consensus is not important	Consensus is important
Source: [33], p. 120.	

Table 3.
General assumptions in uncertainty avoidance.

Masculinity	Femininity
Gender roles should be clearly defined and distinguished	Gender roles should not be clearly defined and distinguished
Men are assertive and dominant	Women are taking care of others
Machismo-exaggerated manliness in men is good	Machismo-exaggerated manliness in men is bad
Men should be decisive	Women should be supportive
Work takes priority over other duties	Private life is important
Advancement, success, and money are important	Good atmosphere at work is important
Source: [33], p. 121.	

Table 4.
General assumptions in masculinity vs. femininity.

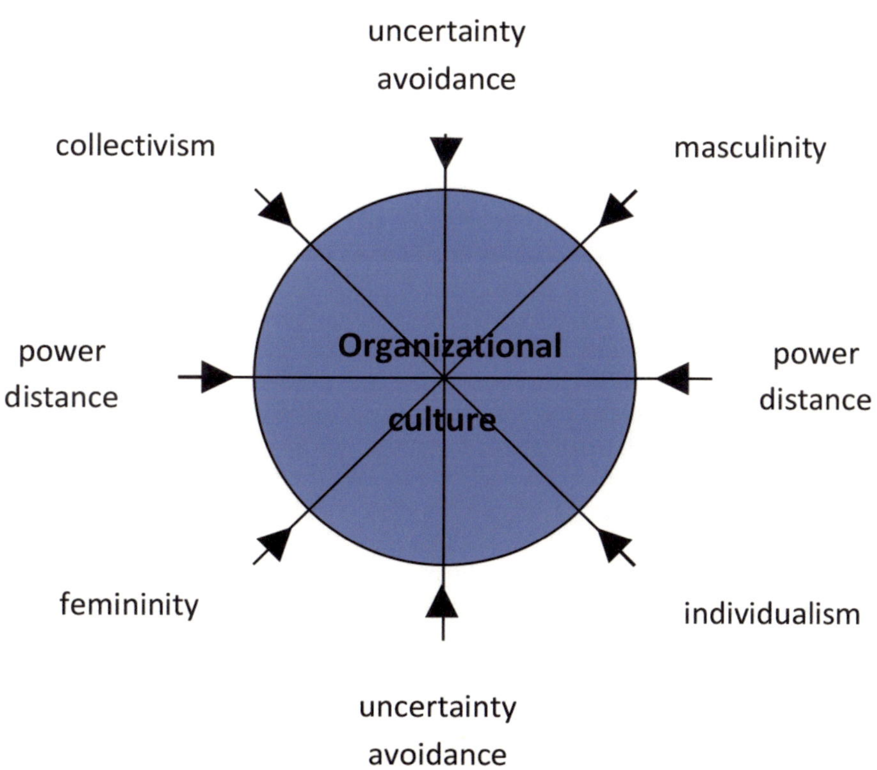

Figure 2.
Model of basic assumptions of organizational culture based on national culture. Source: [4], p. 70

9. Study of basic assumptions in an organizational culture

Within this research, culture (especially its religion component) is treated as an independent variable [34–36]. This research focuses its scope on two organizations in the Podlaskie Voivodship (North-Eastern part of Poland).

Companies in this region operate in religious plurality, which stems from the region's location and history. This diversity allowed for the creation of distinct value systems and attitudes. Nowadays, two largest ethnic groups in the region are the members of the Catholic and Orthodox Churches.

As in 2010, the Voivodship has a population of 11,883 inhabitants [4]. Catholic and Orthodox congregations overall constitute 77 and 13.5% of all inhabitants of Podlaskie Voivodeship, respectively. However, in some areas, the proportions are significantly different. For instance, over 80% of the inhabitants of the Hajnowski district are Orthodox Church believers [37].

9.1 Research sample

The choice of this research sample was purposeful. The comparative study in this research includes two companies. Out of the two researched companies, one is located in a Catholic-surrounding, in a region where 99.7% of the local population declares Catholicism, while the remaining 0.3% declares a different religion or atheism. Contrastingly, the other company is located in an Orthodox environment, where the local population consists of 60.6% Orthodox, 25.3% Catholic and 14.1% other religion inhabitants. The companies employ 300 and 51 workers, respectively.

The number of research participants amounted to 99, out of which 64 participants declared Catholicism, while 35—Orthodox religion. All of the research participants came from religiously homogenous families. The family members of the participant would all declare the same religion as the research participant.

9.2 Research methodology

This research has adopted the case study method, whose design allows to examine the relationship between organizational culture and religion. A questionnaire was used for data collection. It was made of numerous statements embodying the four cultural dimensions. Each of the dimensions was represented by two polarized statements, with a grade scale in between them. The respondent had to use the scale to indicate how accurately a statement illustrated his/her views.

On the left side of the questionnaire, statements expressing individualism, low power distance, low uncertainty avoidance, and masculinity were placed. Contrastingly, the right side of the questionnaire included statements representing expressing collectivism, high power distance, high uncertainty avoidance, and femininity. Research data collection was followed by a statistical analysis, whose aim was to establish whether statistically significant differences occur between the answers collected from the Catholic and Orthodox respondent groups, all the while considering the hypothesis formulated during the course of the research. The U Mann-Whitney test, which is very useful especially in the case of researching small groups, was applied to compare the medians in the two independent research groups.

This research was based on a zero hypothesis—"h0": both research samples derive from a population with the same median. The alternative hypothesis read as follows "h1": research samples derive from varied populations with different medians. The "h0" assumes that no significant differences with regards to the four dimensions of culture occur between the respondents from the Catholic and Orthodox environments. Contrastingly, the alternative hypothesis assumes the opposite, which is that significant differences with regards to the four dimensions of culture do occur between the respondents from the Catholic and Orthodox environments. The results of the research hypothesis analysis suggested rejecting "h0" in favor of "h1."

9.3 Research findings

With regards to the research results, figures depicting influences of basic assumptions of organizational culture have been presented below in **Figure 3**.

The results of the research study confirm that a relatively high level of individualism, relatively low power distance, uncertainty avoidance, and masculinity characterize organizational cultures where the environment is dominated by the Catholic religion. Contrastingly, the organizational culture derived from the Orthodox environment is characterized by a relatively high level of collectivism, femininity, power distance, and the relatively low level of tolerance of uncertainty.

9.4 Verification of the research findings

Following the presented model of organizational culture was the process of verifying the research results. In order to do that, another study of both previously described companies was carried out and was completed by the same group of respondents. The second study aimed to identify differences in cultural assumptions in organizational cultures of both investigated organizations. This study was carried out with the use of a survey, which, as the previous one, included opposing statements and a ranking scale in between each pair. There were eight opposing statements in total: each two regarded one of the four dimensions. This time, the respondent was asked to indicate the extent to which the dimension is present in his/her company. The scale placed in between the opposing statements had 9 points. The grades 1–4, placed near to the statement on the left of the page, would indicate how much this statement depicts the company culture (where "1" would be the highest rank, the fullest compliance and 2–4, respectively, lower). Similarly, the grades 6–9, placed near the statement on the right side of the page, indicated how much that

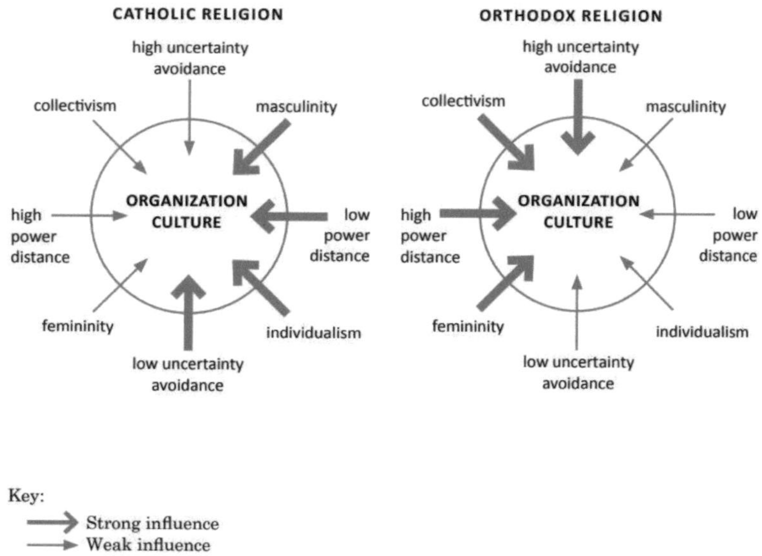

Figure 3.
Models of basic assumptions of organizational culture influenced by religions. Source: [4], p. 125.

statement depicts the company culture (where "9" would be the highest rank, the fullest compliance and 8, 7, 6, respectively, lower). The middle and neutral grade, "5," was to be used if the statements were equally true in relation to the respondent's company. The opposing statements used in the survey follow in **Tables 5–8** below.

Individualism/collectivism was illustrated by the following statements:

Individualism	Collectivism
Employees are looking for challenges at work and they decide how to tackle them	Employees are not looking for challenges at work and do not want the freedom to decide how to tackle them
Employees prefer being a leader and not a regular member of the group	A regular member of the group status is satisfactory enough

Table 5.
General assumptions in individualism *vs.* collectivism *in organizational culture. Source: [4], p. 64.*

Power distance was illustrated by the following statements:

Small power distance	High power distance
Subordinates do not expect detailed instructions from superiors	Subordinates expect detailed instructions from superiors and generally accept them without reservations
If they have reservations, subordinates rather confidently cast doubt about what their superiors asked them to do	Subordinates rather do not question what their superiors asked them to do even if they have certain doubts
Source: [4], p. 65.	

Table 6.
General assumptions in power distance in organizational culture.

Uncertainty avoidance was illustrated by the following statements:

Small uncertainty avoidance	High uncertainty avoidance
Employees are generally willing to take up non-standard actions and superiors gladly accept when it happens	Employees are reluctant to take non-standard measures and superiors do not expect them to
Employees are often nervous or tense at work	Employees are rarely nervous or tense at work
Source: [4], p. 66.	

Table 7.
General assumptions in uncertainty avoidance in organizational culture.

Masculinity/femininity was illustrated by the following statements:

Masculinity	Femininity
Employees expect rapid promotion, non-routine work, high earnings, and recognition from the managers	Nice atmosphere at work, good relationships with colleagues and supervisors, and stable employment is what employees expect of the workplace
The chance of high earnings is ideal	Stable employment is ideal
Source: [4], p. 67.	

Table 8.
General assumptions in masculinity or femininity in organizational culture.

The results of the research confirm the reliability of the proposed models of organizational culture in the environment of the Catholic and Orthodox religions. Additionally, the results confirmed that statistically significant differences with regards to the dimensions expressed by statements from tables above do occur.

The results thereby demonstrate the usefulness and practical aspect of the presented models of organizational culture.

As per the research results, it can be assumed that the organizational culture in companies dominated by the Catholic religion is rather task-orientated while in companies dominated by the Orthodox religion—it is rather relationship orientated. This should serve as an indicator for managers when dealing with subordinates. However, it must be added that despite the differences, there are also numerous similarities bonding the two confessions. Hence, both differences and similarities between the two groups will have an impact on the company culture.

10. Conclusions

Preferences for values and cultural dimensions often stem from religion. It is the sources of guidelines for employees to recall and rely on when making difficult decisions at work. Religion, therefore, proves to be an impactful factor co-creating culture. This is also true in the case of business and organizational culture.

Due to its exceptional influence, organizational culture is one of the most intensely researched concepts within its field. It can influence the behavior of the organization members as well as the performance of the organization as a whole.

No organization and no organizational culture are created in a vacuum or arise from nothingness. The forces external to the organization and its entire environment help shape the culture within. It is the organization's founder, especially in its first stages, who originally builds the organization and its culture. However, as the organization develops, the influence of the environment systematically increases. The exchange with the external environment intensifies, the inflow of new employees increases, and new needs like adapting to changes on the marker, making acquisitions or mergers arise. The external impact, although changing with time, will always remain as one of the culture-producing factors for the organization. Therefore, if the external values of the environment and internal values of employees do not support the organizational culture, there is a risk for the company of not achieving corporate objectives.

The impact of religion on the process of creating organizational culture cannot be overestimated. Based on this research results, conclusions for managers can be drawn. In general, Catholic culture requires more individual motivation and rewards systems, while the Orthodox culture—group motivation and rewards systems. The members of the Catholic organizational culture will prefer a rather flat organizational structure with participating management style while the Orthodox members—rather hierarchical structure with a more directive management style. Similarly, the Catholic culture members will prefer freedom in the way they accomplish tasks, more learning opportunities as well as more challenges at work in general while Orthodox culture members would prefer to fulfill their task in a normalized, routined way, not to have numerous learning opportunities or challenges at work. Additionally, Catholic-influenced organizational culture will be characterized by task orientation and rather rational, based on expertise leadership. Contrastingly, Orthodox-influenced organizational culture will be characterized by relationship orientation and rather mystical, based on formal authority leadership.

Companies operating in a religiously diversified environment face, therefore, a unique opportunity of building organizational culture supportive of those differences. In order to succeed in building and maintaining an organizational culture for varied stakeholders, specific competences are required. Those could be not only knowledge of the customs of a given religion or confession, but, more importantly, subtle skills of social and emotional intelligence like leading by example, openness, acceptance, respect, and inclusivity.

Author details

Barbara Mazur
Faculty of Management, Lublin University of Technology, Poland

*Address all correspondence to: b.mazur@pollub.pl

References

[1] Krasiński M. Kulturowe uwarunkowania wykorzystania japońskich koncepcji, metod i technik zarządzania. Wydawnictwo Uniwersytetu Ekonomicznego: Wrocław; 2014

[2] Hofstede G. Kultury i organizacje. Warszawa: PWE; 2000

[3] Linton R. Kulturowe podstawy osobowości. Warszawa: PWN; 2000

[4] Mazur B. Kultura organizacyjna w zróżnicowanym wyznaniowo otoczeniu. Oficyna Wydawnicza Politechniki Białostockiej: Białystok; 2012

[5] Davie G. Sociology of Religion. Thousand Oaks, CA: Sage; 2007

[6] Parboteeah PK, Paik Y, Cullen JB. Religious groups and work values: A focus on Buddhism, Christianity, Hinduism, and Islam. International Journal of Cross Cultural Management. 2010;**9**(1):51-67

[7] Trompenaars F, Woolliams P. Business across Cultures. Chichester: Capstone Publishing; 2003

[8] Geertz C. Religia jako system kulturowy. In: Mokrzycki E, editor. Racjonalność i styl myślenia. Warszawa: Wydawnictwo IFiS PAN; 1992

[9] Benner DG. Toward the psychology of spirituality: Implication for personality and psychotherapy. Journal of Psychology and Christianity. 1989;**5**:19-30

[10] Mitroff IA, Denton EA. A study of spirituality in the workplace. Sloan Management Review. 1999;**40**(4):83-92

[11] Bjerke B. Kultura a style przywództwa. Oficyna Ekonomiczna: Kraków; 2004

[12] Hofstede G, Hofstede GJ. Cultures and Organizations: Software of the Mind. NewYork: McGraw-Hill; 2005

[13] Konecki K. Nowi pracownicy a kultura organizacyjna. Studium folkloru fabrycznego. Wydawnictwo Uniwersytetu Łódzkiego: Łódź; 1992

[14] Konecki K. Studia z metodologii badań jakościowych. Teoria ugruntowana. Warszawa: PWN; 2000

[15] Cz S. Organizacyjne uczenie się jako forma kształtowania kultury organizacyjnej. In: Sitko-Lutek A, editor. Organizacyjne uczenie się w rozwoju kompetencji przedsiębiorstw. Warszawa: C.H.Beck; 2009

[16] Karczewski L. Etyka biznesu. Kulturowe uwarunkowania. Oficyna Wydawnicza Politechniki Opolskiej: Opole; 2008

[17] Kankaanranta-Jännäri J. The relationship between organizational culture and individual values: A comparative study between Estonia and Finland. In: Vadi M, Reino A, Hämmal G, editors. National and International Aspects of Organizational Culture. Tartu: Tartu University Press; 2006

[18] Schein EH. Organizational Culture and Leadership. San Francisco: Jossey-Bass; 1985

[19] Schein EH. Organizational Culture and Leadership. San Francisco, Washington, London: Jossey-Bass Publisher; 1992

[20] Alvesson M. The play of metaphors. In: Hassard J, editor. Postmodernism and Organizations. London: Sage; 1993

[21] Schultz M. On Studying Organizational Cultures: Diagnosis and Understanding. Berlin: Walter de Gruyter; 1995

[22] Philips ME. Industry as a cultural grouping [thesis]. Los Angeles: University of California; 1990

[23] Alvesson M. Understanding Organizational Culture. London: Sage Publications; 2002

[24] Martin J. Organizational Culture. Mapping the Terrain. Thousand Oaks, London: Sage; 2002

[25] Smircich L. Concepts of culture and organizational analysis. Administrative Science Quarterly. 1993;**28**(3):339-358

[26] Schein EH. Organizational Culture and Leadership. NewYork: John Wiley & Sons; 2004

[27] Meyerson D, Martin J. Cultural change: An integration of three different views. Journal of Management Studies. 1987;**24**(6):623-647

[28] Søndergaard M. Research note: Hofstede's consequences: A study of reviews, citations and replications. Organization Studies. 1994;**15**(3):447-456

[29] Pavett C, Morris T. Management styles within a multinational corporation: A five country comparative study. Human Relations. 1995;**48**(10):1171-1191

[30] Shipper F, Kincaid J, Rotondo DM, Hoffman RC. A cross-cultural exploratory study of the linkage between emotional intelligence and managerial effectiveness. International Journal of Organizational Analysis. 2003;**11**:171-191

[31] Kostera M. Zarządzanie międzykulturowe. In: Koźmiński AK, Piotrowski W, editors. Zarządzanie. Teoria i praktyka. Wydawnictwo Naukowe PWN: Warszawa; 2010

[32] Gahan P, Abeysekera L. What shapes an Individual's work values? An integrated model of the relationship between work values, National Culture and self-construal. International Journal of Human Resource Management. 2009;**20**(1):126-147

[33] Mazur B. Basic assumptions of organizational culture in religiously diverse environments. International Journal of Contemporary Management. 2015;**14**(3):115-132. DOI: 10.4467/24498939IJCM.15.007.4309

[34] Hofstede G. Cultures and Organizations: Software of the Mind. London: McGraw-Hill; 1991

[35] Trompenaars F. Riding the Waves of Culture. London: Books The Economist; 1993

[36] Ralston DA, Holt DH, Terpstra RH, Yu KC. The impact of national culture and economic ideology on managerial work values: A study of the United States, Russia, Japan, and China. Journal of International Business Studies. 1997;**28**(1):177-207

[37] Krzysztofek K, Sadowski A, editors. Pogranicza i multikulturalizm w warunkach Unii Europejskiej: implikacje da wschodniego pogranicza Polski, t.1. Wydawnictwo Uniwersytetu w Białymstoku: Białystok; 2004

Chapter 3

Correlation among Human Resource Flexibility Strategy, Organizational Citizenship Behavior and Organizational Performance in Ecotourism Industry

Ling-Chuan Huang and Ping-Fu Hsu

Abstract

To satisfy the demands for production peak, reduce personnel costs for labor, limit the increase of employees in enterprises, and focus on corporate specialty to develop the competitive advantage, enterprises would generally apply human resource flexibility strategy to achieve the objectives. The practice of human resource flexibility strategy would change work-related characteristics; besides, the effect of the system on employees would decide the effort, absenteeism, or turnover. Aiming at supervisors and employees in ecotourism, as the research objects, a total of 500 copies of questionnaire are distributed, and 351 valid copies are retrieved, with the retrieval rate of 70%. The research results reveal positive and significant effects of 1. human resource flexibility strategy on organizational citizenship behavior, 2. organizational citizenship behavior on organizational performance, and 3. human resource flexibility strategy on organizational performance. According to the results, suggestions are eventually proposed, expecting to provide essential assistance for the human resource flexibility strategy in ecotourism and assist in the sustainable development.

Keywords: ecotourism, human resource flexibility strategy, organizational citizenship behavior, organizational performance

1. Introduction

Tourism industry became a globally economic activity by the end of twentieth century and rapidly developed to become the major industry in the world in the beginning of twenty-first century. Modern people stress more on leisure, and convenient transportation facilitates the tourism market; especially, diverse tour design and service coverage with local characteristics and local culture are enriched and activated. To cope with the above demands, lots of scenic spots, with rural ecological environment and historical and cultural monument, would attract the visit of urban citizens for enjoying the landscape and experiencing local culture. A lot of people therefore pay attention to special travel activity such as ecotourism. The participation in ecotourism and the development of ecotourism activity become the trend. Furthermore, convenient travel information acquisition from the Internet has made the tourism market become more competitive. An enterprise gradually emphasizes the employees' discretionary behavior, due to enhancing visitors' self-awareness and increasing unpredictability in the ecotourism management environment, to cope with changes in external environment and acquire competitive advantage. Conscientiousness, altruism, and active support emphasized in organizational citizenship behavior are the key factors in the effective operation of an organization. Nevertheless, human resource flexibility allows an organization to rapidly make response and adjustment to environmental changes. Facing high uncertainty environment, and globally high competition in the twenty-first century have changed human resource management into an enterprise from one that plays an auxiliary role in the function to one that places equivalent importance on the strategy. The application of human resource strategy flexibility therefore is regarded as a primary direction for organizational flexibility. For instance, job rotation allows employees to receive omnidirectional and multi-cultivation (job flexibility) and choices of salary and diverse welfare decisions (welfare flexibility) as well as understand the relevance between individual and company finance being linked with diverse evaluation methods (salary flexibility). Aiming at human resource flexibility strategy, organizational citizenship behavior, and organizational performance in ecotourism, the research expects to provide essential assistance for the human resource flexibility strategy in ecotourism and assist in the sustainable development.

2. Literature review

2.1 Human resource flexibility strategy

Han et al. [1] defined flexibility as the ability of an enterprise to respond to various requirements in the dynamically competitive environment. Munir and Rahman [2] indicated that human resource flexibility was the human resource management measure taken by an enterprise to cope with the changes in market environment, aiming to stress on labor flexibility, which, with different combination, could generate distinct flexibility effects. Alameddine et al. [3] referred human resource flexibility strategy to flexibly adjust human resource structure, number of employees, job content, working hours, and employees' salary in human resource management to satisfy the requirements of enterprises for different level, different standard, and different model of human resource.

Referring to Do and Yeh [4], four dimensions of job flexibility strategy, time flexibility strategy, quantity flexibility strategy, and salary flexibility strategy are used for the discussion in this study.

1. Job flexibility strategy: Job flexibility strategy refers to employees' mobility and adaptability to execute certain work or task or employing employees with various skills to rapidly respond to the changes in work requirements and technology development.

2. Time flexibility strategy: Time flexibility strategy refers to an enterprise adjusting the time interval or hours in order to match the actual operation requirements or cope with changes in business requirements.

3. Quantity flexibility strategy: Quantity flexibility refers to an enterprise flexibly adjusting the investment in labor to match the fluctuation of market and businesses.

4. Salary flexibility strategy: Most research on salary flexibility involves in changing systematic salary structure to variability in order to fully reflect individual and corporate performance.

2.2 Organizational citizenship behavior

Xu and Li [5] defined organizational citizenship behavior as employees' behaviors exceeding the standard required by the organization; such behaviors were discretionary and not controlled by formal payment systems, including helping colleagues who were behind, maintaining the cleanness of working environment, accepting tasks without complaints, actively accepting undesignated tasks, and proposing suggestions beneficial to the department. Such behaviors were not covered in the formal work statement and were called organizational citizenship behavior [6]. Ross [7] regarded organizational citizenship behavior as individual discretionary behavior, without direct or definite approval of the formal reward system of the organization, to assist organizational functions in effective operation. It was further explained that such discretionary behavior could not be forced to practice through work role requirements or job description, that is, not being restrained through employee contracts [8].

Referring to Tsai et al. [9], organizational citizenship behavior in this study is measured with the following dimensions:

1. Altruism: referring to employees actively helping specific others in the work tasks

2. General compliance: referring to employees' conscientious behavior of actively conforming to the organizational requirements for certain work roles, for example, punctuality, not wasting time, and obedience to rules

2.3 Organizational performance

Chua et al. [10] regarded performance as the standard to measure outcome; when the measured object was an individual, it became job performance, while it was organizational performance when the object was an organization. Jadoo et al. [11] pointed out organizational performance as the measurement of an organization achieving the objective. van der Walt et al. [12] proposed "performance as the measurement of goal attainment of an organization" that could be explained with three points. 1. The measurement of performance was under the premise to confirm organizational objectives. 2. The measurement of performance contained the adoption of measuring methods and the expression of results. 3. The measurement of performance was based on occurred facts, that is, investing resources into an organization and taking outputs as the measurement object.

Referring to Do et al. [13], performance in this study includes three dimensions.

1. Effectiveness: Referring to the comparison of products and services offered by an enterprise with competitors. It is generally measured with sales growth rate and market share.

2. Efficiency: Referring to the ratio of input resources and outputs of an enterprise. It is generally measured with pre-tax income margin or return on investment.

3. Adaptability: Referring to the ability of an enterprise responding to opportunities and threats in the environment, for example, the quantity or sales rate of new products successfully listed in the market in certain period.

2.4 Research hypothesis

Taking employees of high-tech industry in Taiwan as the object, Han et al. [1] found out the direct effect of employees' participation in human resource flexibility systems on organizational citizenship behavior. Coetzee and Stoltz [14] mentioned that the relationship between flexibility and employee behavior lies in flexibility being able to result in consistent common value and behavior of employees through the behavior scripts to enhance efficient internal coordination in the company. Do and Yeh [4] proved the effect of human resource flexibility strategy on employees' work behavior, where the practice of flexible working hours could reduce employees' attendance or enhance the productivity, mainly because the practice of human resource flexibility strategy (e.g., flexible employee training) resulted in positive employment relationship to reduce employees' absence and turnover. In this case, the hypothesis is proposed in this study.

H1: Human resource flexibility strategy shows positive and significant effects on organizational citizenship behavior.

Xu and Li [5] defined organizational citizenship behavior as individual discretionary behavior, which was not directly or definitely related to rewards, but could enhance organizational efficiency, including cooperation with colleagues, executing extra tasks without complaints, keeping time, voluntarily assisting others, efficiently utilizing time, well applying organizational resources, sharing opinions, and positively representing the organization [11]. Tsai et al. [9] revealed that organizational performance relied on the full support and devotion of all employees in the organization; a leader should construct employees' professional and leading ability, empower employees in the professional field, excite employees' activeness, and induce employees' organizational citizenship behavior to enhance organizational performance and be willing to share leaders' responsibilities. Accordingly, the hypothesis is proposed in this study.

H2: Organizational citizenship behavior reveals positive and remarkable effects on organizational performance.

Chua et al. [10] proposed the largest positive effect of job flexibility on soft performance (referring to patient satisfaction, medical service quality, professional development of members in departments, and employee satisfaction) to effectively promote organizational performance. Lúanaigh and Hughes [15] indicated that employees with proper autonomy of time would have higher satisfaction to further enhance the organizational performance. Do et al. [13] stated that an enterprise need not pay extra welfare expenses for non-typical workers of temporary staff and outsourcers that it could control the costs and effectively promote the organizational performance. Way et al. [16] proposed the maximal effect of human resource salary flexibility on employees' average monthly productivity that the higher salary flexibility would show better soft performance and higher average monthly production amount to effectively enhance organizational performance. As a result, the hypothesis is proposed in this study.

H3: Human resource flexibility strategy appears positive and notable effects on organizational performance.

3. Sample and measurement indicator

3.1 Research sample and object

Aiming at supervisors and employees in ecotourism as the research object, a total of 500 copies of questionnaire are distributed, and 351 valid copies are retrieved, with the retrieval rate of 70%.

3.2 Test of reliability and validity

Confirmatory factor analysis (CFA) is regarded as an important part in SEM. For this reason, the measurement model should be tested before the two-stage model correction for evaluating the structural model with CFA. When the measured model fit is acceptable, the second step of SEM evaluation is preceded. When preceding CFA, it reveals the standards of the factor loadings of the dimensions in .60–.90, the component reliability in .75–.90, and the average variance extracted in .60–.80. The followings are observed: 1. the factor loadings are higher than .5; 2. the component reliability is higher than .6; and 3. the average variance extracted is higher than .5, conforming to the standards that the dimensions present convergent validity.

4. Empirical result analysis

4.1 Structural model analysis

Structural model analysis covers the model fit analysis and the explanatory power of the overall research model. For this reason, seven numerical indices, referring to researchers' opinions, are used for testing the overall model fit in this study, including chi-square (χ^2) test, χ^2-degree of freedom ratio, fit index and adjusted fit index, root mean square error, comparative fit indices, comparative hypothesis model, and chi-square difference of independent model. The overall result analyses are organized in **Table 1**.

From previous overall model fit indices, there is favorable goodness-of-fit between the structured model and the observation data, revealing that the theoretical model could fully explain the observation data. In this case, the correlation coefficient and correlation estimate of human resource flexibility strategy to organizational citizenship behavior and organizational performance could be further understood after the model fit test.

The research data, organized in **Table 2**, reveal good preliminary fit of the overall model.

In regard to internal fit, human resource flexibility strategy presents positive and significant correlations with organizational citizenship behavior (0.82, $p < 0.01$), organizational citizenship behavior shows positive and remarkable correlations with organizational performance (0.88, $p < 0.01$), and human resource flexibility strategy also shows positive and notable correlations with organizational performance (0.83, $p < 0.01$) that H1, H2, and H3 are supported.

Fit indices	Allowable limit	This research model	Model fit judgment
χ^2 (Chi-square)	The smaller the better	16.75	
χ^2-degree of freedom ratio	<3	1.84	Conformed
GFI	>.9	0.97	Conformed
AGFI	>.8	0.84	Conformed
RMSEA	<.08	0.03	Conformed
CFI	>.9	0.92	Conformed
NFI	>.9	0.90	Conformed

Table 1.
Fit analysis of the research model.

Evaluation item			Result
Preliminary fit internal fit		Job flexibility strategy	0.75**
		Time flexibility strategy	0.67*
		Quantity flexibility strategy	0.63*
		Salary flexibility strategy	0.70**
	Organizational citizenship behavior	Altruism	0.74**
		General compliance	0.72**
	Organizational performance	Effectiveness	0.73**
		Efficiency	0.76**
			0.71**
	Source flexibility strategy → organizational citizenship behavior		0.82**
	Organizational citizenship behavior → organizational performance		0.88**
	Human resource flexibility strategy → organizational performance		0.83**

*Note: *Stands for $p < 0.05$, **for $p < 0.001$.*

Table 2.
Overall linear structural model analysis result.

5. Conclusion

The research results reveal significantly positive correlations between ecotourism human resource flexibility strategy, organizational citizenship behavior, and organizational performance. The higher application of human resource flexibility strategy would show better organizational performance to enhance employees' organizational citizenship behavior. Especially in job rotation and multi-skill training, human resource flexibility strategy in ecotourism allows employees to engage in various works and learn new work contents. Employees being able to undertake different positions in different departments would understand the details of work execution processes, mainly because the participation process could induce the activeness and enhance the organizational citizenship behavior. Furthermore, human resource flexibility strategy in ecotourism contains the encouragement of increasing resource distribution. For instance, multi-skill training is the performance of employees being emphasized in ecotourism to enhance the organizational citizenship behavior and promote organizational performance.

6. Suggestion

From the research results and findings, the following practical suggestions are proposed in this study:

1. According to the requirement for organizational development, ecotourism is suggested to plan and cultivate professional skills and talents required for the organizational development. The flexible arrangement of job flexibility could be enhanced and human resource development could be more positively planned through systematical education training or planning of other learning opportunities (e.g., job rotation, project organization, or cross-department work team).

2. Ecotourism businesses should stress on the effect of salary system and salary structure on the organization and employees, properly change salary payment reference, increase the linkage between salary, employee performance, and employee skills, and enhance the flexibility ratio. Moreover, the connection between salary and strategic objective of ecotourism should be positively taken into account to encourage employees' work motivation as well as promote organizational performance and employees' organizational citizenship behavior.

3. Salary flexibility in ecotourism aims to have employees realize the relevance between salary and operation conditions of the company. The employees would present organizational citizenship behavior when the company could clearly deliver, explain, and describe the fair methods.

Author details

Ling-Chuan Huang[1] and Ping-Fu Hsu[2*]

1 Dayen University of PH. D. Program in Management, Taiwan, R. O. C.

2 Ming Dao University, Taiwan, R. O. C.

*Address all correspondence to: joey5621@mdu.edu.tw

References

[1] Han K, Trinkoff AM, Gurses AP. Work-related factors, job satisfaction and intent to leave the current job among United States nurses. Journal of Clinical Nursing. 2015;**24**(21-22):3224-3232

[2] Munir RIS, Rahman RA. Determining dimensions of job satisfaction using factor analysis. Procedia Economics and Finance. 2016;**37**:488-496

[3] Alameddine M, Bauer JM, Richter M, Sousa-Poza A. Trends in job satisfaction among German nurses from 1990 to 2012. Journal of Health Services Research & Policy. 2016;**21**(2):101-108

[4] Do B, Yeh PW. Role of human resource flexibility in organizational innovation. Tunghai Management Review. 2016 in Press

[5] Xu M, Li SX. Analysis of good practice of public health emergency operations centers. Asian Pacific Journal of Tropical Medicine. 2015;**8**(8):677-682

[6] Alghamdi MG. Nursing workload: A concept analysis. Journal of Nursing Management. 2016;**24**(4):449-457

[7] Ross A. Innovating Professional Services: Transforming Value and Efficiency. Farnham, UK: Gower Publishing Ltd.; 2015

[8] Hayes AF. An index and test of linear moderated mediation. Multivariate Behavioral Research. 2015;**50**:1-22

[9] Tsai KH, Liao YC, Hsu TT. Does the use of knowledge integration mechanisms enhance product innovativeness? Industrial Marketing Management. 2015;**46**:214-223

[10] Chua RYJ, Roth Y, Lemoine JF. The impact of culture on creativity: How cultural tightness and cultural distance affect global innovation crowdsourcing work. Administrative Sciences Quarterly. 2015;**60**:189-227

[11] Jadoo SAA, Aljunid SM, Dastan I, Tawfeeq RS, Mustafa MA, Ganasegeran K, et al. Job satisfaction and turnover intention among Iraqi doctors—A descriptive cross-sectional multicentre study. Human Resources for Health. 2015;**13**(21)

[12] van der Walt F, Thasi ME, Jonck P. Skills shortages and job satisfaction—Insights from the gold-mining sector of South Africa. African Journal of Business and Economic Research. 2016;**11**(1):143-183

[13] Do B, Yeh PW, Madsen J. Exploring the relationship among human resource flexibility, organizational innovation and adaptability culture. Chinese Management Studies. 2016;**10**(4):657-674

[14] Coetzee M, Stoltz E. Employees' satisfaction with retention factors: Exploring the role of career adaptability. Journal of Vocational Behavior. 2015;**89**:83-91

[15] Lúanaigh PÓ, Hughes F. The nurse executive role in quality and high performing health services. Journal of Nursing Management. 2016;**24**(1):132-136

[16] Way SA, Tracey JB, Fay CH, Wright PM, Snell SA, Chang S, et al. Validation of a multidimensional HR flexibility measure. Journal of Management. 2015;**41**(4):1098-1131

Chapter 4

Zionist Organizations in Voronezh

Bakhtin Viktor Viktorovich and Ashmarov Igor' Anatol'yevich

Abstract

The chapter is based on materials from the archives and investigations of the OGPU of the late 1920s and early 1930s. The last years of the XIX century and the first twentieth century became a time of rapid development and strengthening of the Zionist movement in Russia developed rapidly. In 1902, over a thousand disparate Zionist organizations merged into the Russian Zionist Organization (RNO). In this article, we will consider the processes taking place in a separate region of Russia - the Central Black Earth Region (CCO). Voronezh became the center of the Central Council in 1928.

Keywords: political regime, Zionism

1. Introduction

In the late 1920s, the Soviet political regime acquired the features of totalitarianism, which D. Volkogonov described as "classical Stalinism" [1]. Its formation took place under the conditions of the formation of a one-party system with increased repression against dissidents.

Soviet society reacted to the tightening of the regime by various forms of protests: from domestic anti-Sovietism to armed uprisings. Resistance to totalitarianism in Soviet Russia was massive. The forced establishment of a one-party wild tattoo in the early 1920s destroyed the possibility of legal struggle.

In pre-revolutionary Russia, Zionism, the Jewish national movement, aimed at the unification and revival of the Jewish people in their historical homeland - in Eretz-Israel, as well as the ideological concept on which this movement is based, arose.

In May 1918, the Central Committee of the North Ossetia officially declared its neutrality in matters of domestic Russian politics. The main goal of the Zionist groups operating at that time in the USSR was agitation among Jews in favor of resettlement in Palestine and preparation of young Zionists for labor activity [2].

Since July 1919, the Soviet authorities launched a widespread attack on the Zionist movement. By 1923, only two authorized Zionist organizations remained in the Soviet Union: the Jewish Communist Workers Party Poalei Zion (created on the basis of the Jewish Social Democratic Party Poalei Zion) and the so-called "legal" wing of Khe-Halutz, whose supporters considered coexistence possible Zionist movement with the Soviet regime.

In 1926, arrests of Zionist activists began in different parts of the country [3]. In April 1927, the NKVD of the USSR called for the liquidation of Khe-Halutz because the latter "in addition to ... the tasks of attracting Jews to work is also engaged in the training of construction workers Center in Palestine and facilitates the emigration of Jews to Palestine" [4].

On May 24, 1928, the Politburo of the Central Committee of the All-Union Communist Party of Bolsheviks approved a resolution of the Organizing Bureau of May 21, 1928 on the need to liquidate the legally existing party of the Jewish Communist Party (ETUC). In accordance with this decision, on the night of June 25–26, 1928, the OGPU carried out a special operation to liquidate the ETUC and all its structural divisions. As a result, by the end of the 1920s. Zionism in Russia as a mass movement was suppressed [5].

These are facts illustrating the suppression of the opposition, on the scale of the USSR. In terms of its size, the Central Election Center exceeded a number of European states. The territory of the region amounted to 192 thousand square kilometers, on which more than 11 million people lived [6].

The territorial basis of the Central Black Sea region was: Voronezh, Kursk, Oryol and Tambov provinces, Rannenbursky district of Ryazan province and part of the Efremov district of Tula province. The region was homogeneous in terms of ethnic composition: Russians made up 85%, Ukrainians - 15%, other nationalities - 1% [7].

Jews in large numbers appeared in the Central Black Earth cities during the First World War as refugees. In 1917, according to the census of the Voronezh Jewish Committee for Assistance to War Victims, 6946 Jews lived in Voronezh, of which 4307 were refugees [8–11].

The appearance of Jews in the cities of the Central Black Sea region contributed to the emergence of legal and illegal organizations and institutions. By the end of the 1920s, virtually all Jewish organizations in the city were closed.

Political parties were the first to disappear, the Bund self-destructed, the Poalei Zion club was forcibly closed back in 1921. Heder was eliminated in 1922 as part of the fight against clericalism, a Jewish school I level "due to lack of funds" in 1923, the orphanage, since it "did not have its own production base and school" was merged with the commune school [12].

In 1927, the pro-government Committee for the Land Management of Working Jews (KOMZET) and the Society for the Land Organization of Working Jews (OZET) were organized in Voronezh, 13 which, among other things, sought to divert the attention of Jews from the Zionist program of creating a "Jewish national center" in Palestine [13, 14].

2. Methodology

The study is based on traditional historical methods. The historical-systemic method was used to study the emergence of the Jewish population in Voronezh, the emergence of Zionist organizations, and analyzed the organizational structures, internal and external relations.

Features of scientific research can be analyzed using the method of scientific objectivity and historicism, which allowed us to identify features of the political views of members of Zionist organizations. Archive-investigative cases are a complex and contradictory historical source, since along with reliable facts and information, they often also contain falsified employees of punitive bodies. In this connection, it is necessary to be especially critical of the materials of the investigation and the indictment. But, in our opinion, given that these cases were directed against the exiles, that is, using the terminology of that period, to persons who showed their hostile essence, the fabricated material in them was insignificant or minimal.

The cases also contain ego-documents: letters, photographs, which also allow characterizing political and public views.

The article uses a comparative historical method that allows one to trace the change in state policy in relation to the Zionist movement, to find out the change in the aspects of the interaction of socialist Zionist organizations and Soviet power in different historical periods.

The statistical method made it possible to confirm the analysis of the Zionist population based on the materials of the regional archive. The method of socio-psychological analysis was used and allowed to show the socio-political views of the Zionists, their moods.

The use of various approaches and methods of scientific research allowed us to study the activities of two organizations in respect of which repression was applied.

3. Results

Arrests of Zionists in different regions of the country led to an unexpected result. Voronezh has become a place of concentration of members of various Zionist parties and organizations, whose term of administrative exile expired. Some of the Zionists filed applications to leave for Palestine, the request was granted to 21 people who left Voronezh.

On August 18, 1930, OGPU officers in Voronezh carried out mass searches of 30 Zionists, 20 of them were arrested [15]. Thus, investigative file No. 6991 of the "Zionist organization in the city of Voronezh" arose. 19 people were charged, and the case was dismissed for one arrested. According to the investigation, all of them "were hostile to the Soviet power and the dictatorship of the proletariat, set themselves the task of fighting the existing state system" [16].

Employees of the punitive body in Voronezh "received" fertile material, since all those involved in the Zionist case had already been harassed and were serving a sentence or imprisonment. 12 defendants were members of the illegal Zionist Socialist Party (TS), 6 belonged to the youth Zionist socialist organization "Gasmer-Gatsior" and one belonged to the youth Zionist organization "Khe-Halutz."

An analysis of the biographies of those arrested made it possible to single out the dynamics of repressions, as it was first convicted in 1924–4 people, in 1925–5, 1926–8, in 1927–1, and in 1928–1. Most were arrested for belonging to Zionist organizations in Ukraine, others in Moscow, Lenin-grad and Rostov. By gender and age characteristics: 13 men and 5 women, the oldest was 49 years old, the youngest was 20 years old. The average age is 25–30 years.

According to investigators, "members of Zionist parties and organizations ... made up organizations for anti-Soviet purposes and conducted activities aimed at combating the Soviet power" [17]. It can be safely assumed that the Zionists who found themselves in Voronezh were real opponents of Stalinism and the case materials reflected their real socio-political views.

During interrogations, they expressed their views on the ongoing political processes in the USSR. These views, obtained during the investigation, reflect the evolution of many romantics of the revolution, who, with enthusiasm, having met the overthrow of the monarchy and the beginning of radical social transformations, gradually became disappointed in the post-revolutionary reality.

In the context of a tightening of the political regime, suppression of all opposition in the country, and the beginning of violent collectivization, a transformation of the socio-political views of the social Zionists took place. They believed that the October Revolution of 1917 as a revolution was not completed, "a revolution in which, instead of tsarist power and the power of the Provisional Government, the oppression of the Bolshevik dictatorship was established." A member of the Central

Committee, David Brailovsky, 18, who was the leader of the Voronezh Zionist community, compared Stalinism with the bureaucratic regime or Bonapartist dictatorship [18, 19]. Such a comparison was a fairly common comparison in the 1920s and was present in many theoretical and journalistic works [20].

Anatoly Ovseevich, 21 former student of the Leningrad Institute of National Economy, characterized the regime as "fascist" [21, 22].

Such a comparison has not yet become widespread among the socialist milieu, but has been common among anarchists. One of the first to pay attention to many of the most important features of totalitarianism was liberal and anarchist theorists.

So, even at the II Congress of the Anarcho-Syndicalist International - the International Association of Workers (MAT) in 1925, the Italian Armando Borgi compared Mussolini's fascist regime with Bolshevism [23]. Perhaps A. Ovseyevich was familiar with some anarcho-syndicalists and borrowed from them this is a comparison. He could get acquainted with the left-wing radical criticism of totalitarianism, both in the Ural exile and in Voronezh itself, where many anarchists ended the administrative exile [24].

The link of the 1920s contributed to the synthesis of the ideas of various political parties that were in opposition to the existing government.

During the searches, a number of manuscript works were discovered, many of which formed the basis of the prosecution. During an interrogation on August 27, 1930, David Brailovsky said: "I refuse to give evidence about the author of the thesis of the CSP and the article 'Our Disagreements', as well as generally to give testimonies. I also refuse to testify about the persons from whom I received 2 books of Borokhov [25] in Hebrew, published in Warsaw in 1926 and 1927.

I admit that the above-mentioned manuscripts: theses and article are written in my handwriting" [26].

D. Brailovsky believed that in the modern, transitional period, the need arose to unite the Jewish masses through the creation of a labor party, the role of which is played by the CSP. It is she who, "when she appears, is the first intuitively brilliant form" [27].

In his notes, also discovered during the search, Mark Komissarov [28] developed ideas about the illegitimacy of the dictatorship of the Communist Party: "the power of the proletariat as a class should be the power recognized by the majority of the population." [29].

Of particular concern was the practice of deprivation of electoral rights, which is widely used against certain categories of the population in the USSR. This form of socio-economic discrimination was criticized: "the management of the state and society on the basis of political powerlessness of all non-proletarian sections of the population ... should come into irreconcilable conflict with the tasks of social transformation" [30].

Zoya Gilodi [31], being exiled for belonging to Gashomer-Gatsair, worked as a librarian in Voronezh, where she could calmly study literature. She analyzed the work of V. Lenin, "The Collapse of the Second International" [32]. In this case, according to the investigation, she tried to prove that Lenin is a false Marxist [33]. Although in the synopsis she writes a little differently: "Lenin's doctrine is a variant of Marxism," which is not at all It was not a counter-revolutionary statement, since after the death of Lenin in 1924, Soviet party functionaries started talking about Marxism-Leninism.

However, investigators found in Zoe Gilodi even more seditious remarks about Lenin: "Lenin is far from a popular writer ... you must have a more or less solid baggage of knowledge in order to be able to distinguish Lenin's opinion from pure followers of Marxism. Lenin chose a way to strike at the feelings of the townsfolk" [34].

The evolution of the individual views of Zoe Gilodi was also characteristic of the ideological searches of Gashomer-Gatsair. In the 1920s the platform of organization ideology close to communism underwent changes, becoming a synthesis of Zionism with socialism, of Halutianism with the class struggle. When Histadrut was founded [35], Gashomer-Gatsair did not enter any of the political parties operating then in the country, declared himself an independent group [36].

Zionists often held political discussions in their apartments. The limited financial resources of the administratively exiled forced to rent apartments together. So, in one apartment, 6 people lived together.

The Voronezh Zionists also created a mutual assistance fund for material assistance to needy members in Voronezh and other cities [37]. A library was also organized. Conversations, joint readings of the literature led to various discussions. Witnesses in the case, and possibly informants, showed that in the apartments where the Zionists lived, they often read books and talked on different topics. One witness K. testified that in the evenings, 5–6 people gathered at Brailovsky almost every day, and twice - about 12–15 people gathered. "During their disputes, they spoke exclusively in Hebrew, the conversation was very noisy, you could hear them trying to prove something to others" [38].

According to testimony, many Zionists openly criticized the existing system. In particular, Ovseyevich stated that the dispossession policy that the Bolsheviks began to pursue was "a method of physically and administratively protecting the kulaks, not a political measure," [39] and the chronic shortage of essential goods was a consequence of the "ongoing intensified industrialization of the country" [40].

The presence of various handwritten works was a reflection of political censorship. The strengthening of state ideology led to an increase in prohibited literature, and in addition there was a shortage of books and periodicals. All this gave rise in Soviet conditions to the appearance of a self-publishing house - as a way of unofficial, uncensored production and distribution of literary works, religious and journalistic texts.

Zionists copied many publications from each other, handed over to their friends. Anatoly Ovseevich organized a library, where in addition to both legal and forbidden literature was collected, it is presented both in print and in manuscript form. Ovseyevich ordered books to cousin Kransky, who lives in Berlin. The books were translated from German into Russian by Ovseevich and Brailovsky into Russian, and then a handwritten translation was distributed among the Zionists of Voronezh. According to the investigation, Ovseyevich translated "The Worldview of Capitalism" [41] Otto Bauer [42], Brailovsky - the book "Implementation of Economic Activities" [43] Fritz Naftali [44] and the report "Transformation of Capitalism" by Werner Zombat [45]. The latter is of particular interest, so most likely the handwritten translation "The Transformation of Capitalism" could be a variant of the newspaper or magazine publication of Zombat and had a free translation of the title of the future book "The Fate of Capitalism" [46].

The investigation could not establish the authorship of two manuscripts [47]. It is known from the documents of the case that "Industrial Policy of the USSR" is Ovseevich's manuscript [48], it is not clear whether he was his work of authorship, or a translation, or is it just a rewritten work of some author.

The manuscript "The Economics of the Jewish Proletariat and National Competition" was discovered during a search of Maria Halperina, which she received from some Zionist whom she does not remember [49].

OGPU employees also seized numerous letters from Palestine, which were preserved and attached to the case as material evidence. The letters themselves are also valuable sources on the history of the Zionist movement in Soviet Russia, and also contain information about the structure of the first settlers in Palestine. These Letters were interpreted as "written directives of the Zionist leadership" or "coordination of anti-Soviet activities" of Zionists in the USSR [50].

December 30, 1930 was sentenced to the Voronezh Zionists. From the conviction of case No. 6991: "they all lived in Voronezh, Jews, citizens of the RSFSR, former petty bourgeois, now servants, were convicted of anti-Soviet activities, completely exposed that, while in the city of Voronezh

1. created a Zionist organization, which sets as its task the fight against Soviet power and the change in the existing state system;

2. established contact with foreign and Zionist organizations in other cities;

3. carried out work to raise the political level of members of their organization;

4. organized an illegal library, supplied with foreign party literature, not allowed for distribution in USSR;

5. distributed illegal printed and handwritten anti-Soviet materials;

6. organized a mutual assistance fund for material assistance to needy members of the organization in the city of Voronezh, as well as members of Zionist organizations in other cities.

7. conducted anti-Soviet agitation among residents of the city of Voronezh" [51].

19 people were sentenced to various terms of imprisonment under charges under Art. 58–10 (propaganda or agitation containing a call to overthrow, undermine or weaken the Soviet power or to commit certain counter-revolutionary crimes, as well as distribution or production, or storage of literature of the same content) and 58–11 (all kinds of organizational activities aimed at preparing or committing counter-revolutionary crimes provided for in this chapter) of the Criminal Code of the RSFSR. The case against the ongoing Gogol case in Israel was dismissed, four went to Palestine - Mendel Rogovoy, Meer Segal, Berta Movshovich, Abraham Uchitel.

The case against 7 Voronezh Zionists was set aside for department production: Aizik Furman, Rachel Sukhenka, Boris Genin, Chaim Livshits, Samuel Stern, Moses Shulman, Rachel Feld-man [52].

In 1930, arrests were carried out among a large Voronezh colony of exiled Social Democrats (Mensheviks). In this case, Rosa Levit (Levina) [53], who was involved in the case as a Zionist, was convicted. She was accused of "being a member of an active group of exiled Mensheviks in Voronezh and actively participating in the activities of the illegal mutual assistance fund, collecting membership fees to the fund." Levin openly criticized the repressive policies of the Stalinist regime. She condemned the open trial of the Fedorovites [54]: "The verdict of the court on the shooting of 16 defendants is unusually cruel, the court is not fair, such sentences are handed down to the peasants that are inconsistent with the case, since the court did not prove that they really (i.e., Fedorov's) are counterrevolutionary organization [55].

Levina criticized the policy of forced collectivization: "The Soviet government is conducting a wrong policy towards the peasantry, dispossessing not only the kulak, but also the middle peasant" [56]. This phrase was introduced into the indictment on the basis of testimony, in connection with which falsification of these testimonies is possible, so Rosa Levit (Levina) did not plead guilty to anti-Soviet activities, but refused to answer a number of questions.

In 1932, members of the Gashomer-Gatsior were arrested again. The movement was founded in 1916 as a Jewish counterpart to scout organizations. The purpose of which was to prepare Jewish youth for resettlement in Eretz Yisrael. The principles of socialist Zionism, combining Zionism and Social Democracy, were declared as the basic values of the movement.

According to the investigation, the exiled Zionists, retaining their previous political views, created an organization in Voronezh under the leadership of Aizik Furman [57], which was held in case No. 6991.

From the indictment: "going to the apartments, we discussed the political measures of the Soviet government and the CPSU (b) and worked out a counter-revolutionary program that was put into practice."

The exiled Zionist Naum Breitman [58], member of the Odessa group, worked at the Stalin plant. The assignment to the plant of the name of the party leader was already a symbol of the forming personality cult. It was built for the manufacture of cables by the industrialist A.N. Petichev in 1916 during the First World War. Revolutionary processes and subsequent nationalization halted production. In 1928, the plant was converted for the production of agricultural machinery. In October 1930, the plant was named after Joseph Stalin.

In March 1932, Breutmann organized the "Italian strike" [59], in which 5 enumerated workers of the factory department took part. The day before they filed for dismissal. The reason is extremely low wages. The management of the plant did not sign, as "there was an urgent need for accountants." And as a result - the Italian strike, which lasted from March 24 to 26, 1932.

On March 26, the factory committee convened a general meeting of accountants, at which the chief accountant of the plant reported. Breitman openly stated at the meeting that salaries were unrealistic and demanded an increase based on the calculation of increasing market prices. As a result, "with his speech, Breitman caused anti-Soviet activity by counting workers, as a result of which the meeting was disrupted and the factory committee did not achieve its goals" [60]. The charge was built on the basis of the meeting's protocols and statements of the plant's administration, which were at the disposal of the investigator. Perhaps it was precisely the appeal of the plant's administration that served as the basis for initiating proceedings against Breitman and served as the basis for the arrests of exiled members of "Gasmer-Gatsior" in Voronezh.

At the interrogation, Naum Breitman said: "By my political convictions, I am a Social Democrat. I sympathize with the ideas of proletarian Zionism. I do not share the policies and measures of the CPSU (b) and the Soviet regime because they contradict my convictions" [61].

In general, he outlined the official program of the organization. September 23, 1932 by the Decree of the OGPU OGPU Aizik Furman, Naum Breutman, Boris Enin [62], Yudif Khaimovich [63] Samuel Stern [64], Israel Bergman [65], Solomon Popel [66] were sent for 3 years.

4. Discussion

Voronezh province was not a territory with the traditional residence of Jews. The emergence of the Voronezh Jewish community was examined by historian A.N. Akinshin [67] and the chief rabbi of Voronezh [68]. In the 19th century, there were 2277 Jews in the province. The problem of the origin of the Zionist movement in the region still remains a "blank spot," and the Jewish political and non-political organizations and associations have not been subjected to scientific research [69]. Meanwhile, the activities of Israel Rozov, one of the leaders of Zionism in Russia, are connected with Voronezh [70].

The emergence of a large Jewish community during the First World War occurred during the massive forced deportation of Jews from the western provinces of the Russian Empire. For Soviet historiography, the topic of Jewish refugee was closed for many years. In contemporary Russian and foreign historiography, there is a steady interest in the problem of refugee, in general, and Jewish refugee during the First World War. Historian I. Belova cites material and Jewish refugee in the Voronezh province [71].

The activities of Jewish public organizations are characterized by M. Zlatina [72], A. Tumanova [73], V. Bakhtin.

However, we have to admit that a comprehensive monograph on the issue of Jewish refugee in Russia during the First World War was not published in the post-Soviet period, historians consider the problem of the process of Jewish refugee in the indicated period only in fragmentary (territorial or other particular aspects) [74].

The topic of the role of the Zionist movement in the political life of the country in the early Soviet period is also a poorly studied historical science. Considering that by 1917 the Zionist organization in Russia had more than 300 thousand members and had a significant impact on the Jewish masses, especially in the areas of the former Pale of Settlement [75]. And we can safely say that among the thousands of Jewish refugees Zionists arrived in Voronezh.

At the end of the 20th century, in the second half of the 1990s, works began to appear in Russia that objectively examined the history of the Zionist movement in Soviet Russia. These include M. Agapov [76], M. Krapivin [77] and others [78].

Despite the discovery of many sources on the history of the Zionist movement in Soviet Russia, nevertheless, on the whole this problem is poorly studied, since it included various trends and movements, including socialist ones, which need further research.

In foreign historiography, the topic of the Jewish socialist movement began to be studied, under certain circumstances, earlier than in the USSR.

Explored various aspects of Nora Levin [79], J. Hen-Tov [80] and others [81].

Of great importance for this issue is the collective work of Boris Morozov and Ziv Galili, "Exiled in Palestine: Emigration of Zionist Convicts from the Soviet Union, 1924–1934 [82].

B. Morozov in a separate article carries out a rigorous analysis of the archives of Russia, Ukraine, Israel, cites sources and statistical materials about those who were deported to Palestine. A group portrait of exiled Zionists, on the basis of a file cabinet compiled by B. Morozov, is of particular research interest [83]. And its further study is possible only with a comprehensive study of the archives of both central and regional Russia, Ukraine, Belarus and Israel, the UK and other countries.

5. Conclusion

Illegal Zionist organizations in Voronezh were defeated. Their specificity was that they consisted of serving a link. We have not yet identified Zionist organizations represented by Jews, natives of the Voronezh region. The only Zionist is a native of Voronezh Popel. However, further research in the archives may reveal new data on the history of Zionist organizations in Voronezh. Illegal Zionist organizations in Voronezh were defeated.

Their specificity was that they consisted of serving a link. We have not yet identified Zionist organizations represented by Jews, natives of the Voronezh region.

The only Zionist is a native of Voronezh Popel. However, further research in the archives may reveal new data on the history of Zionist organizations in Voronezh.

Mass arrests of members of various Zionist parties and movements in the USSR took place in 1937 in accordance with the operative order of the People's Commissar of Internal Affairs of the USSR № 00447 "On the operation to repress former fists, criminals and other anti-Soviet elements."

Mass arrests of members of various Zionist parties and movements in the USSR took place in 1937 in accordance with the operative order of the People's Commissar of Internal Affairs of the USSR № 00447 "On the operation to repress former fists, criminals and other anti-Soviet elements." Many Zionists were again arrested, and convicted as Morduh Shliomovich or shot as Abraham Weinstein, Boris Halperin. The fate of the rest of the Zionists who were involved in Voronezh affairs remains unclear.

Author details

Bakhtin Viktor Viktorovich* and Ashmarov Igor' Anatol'yevich*
Voronezh State Institute of Arts, Russia

*Address all correspondence to: vvbakhtin@rambler.ru and dobrinka75@mail.ru

References

[1] Volkogonov, D.A. Stalinism: essence, genesis, evolution//Actual problems of recent history/Ed. G.N. Sevostyanov. Moscow: Prosveshcheniye, 1991. P. 20.

[2] Agapov, M.G. Party-Soviet leadership and Russian Zionists: in search of modus vivendi (1917-1920s) // Socium and power. 2012. No. 1. Pp. 112, 115.

[3] Kostyrchenko, G.V. Stalin's secret policy: power and anti-Semitism. M.: International Relations, 2001. Pp. 71.75.

[4] Agapov, M.G. Party-Soviet leadership and Russian Zionists: in search of modus vivendi (1917-1920s) // Socium and power. 2012. No. 1. P. 116.

[5] Ibid. P. 116.

[6] Central Black Earth Region: Pocket Guide / comp. V.P. Bayev, A.G. Brown, L.N. Sokolova; open ed. V.N. Alekseev. Voronezh: Commune, 1933.S. 21.

[7] Ibid. P.22.

[8] Korotun, S.N. National minorities of the Voronezh region in 1917-1941: monograph / S.N. Korotun, S.P. Tolkacheva, E.A. Shevchenko. Voronezh: Voronezh State Pedagogical University, 2012. P. 228.

[9] State Archive of the Social and Political History of the Voronezh Region (hereinafter - GAOPI VO). F. 1. Op. 1. D. 431. L.1

[10] Ibid. D. 1055. L.7.

[11] Ibid. L.8.

[12] State Archive of the Voronezh Region (GAVO). F. 10. Op. 1. D. 1886. L. 18.

[13] GARF. F.R. 9498. Op. 1. D. 172. L. 1.

[14] Agapov, M.G. "The struggle for the soul of the Jewish people": Birobidzhan VS. Palestine // Questions of World History. 2010.V. 12. Pp. 130-138

[15] GAOPI VO. F. 9353. Op. 2. D.P. - 26427V.1., L.164.

[16] Ibid. L.246.

[17] GAOPI VO. F. 9353. Op. 2. D.P. - 26427V.1. L.245

[18] Brailovsky David Naftulevich (He is Halperin Moses Yakovlevich) (1893, the city of Chicherin, Kiev province -?). Member of the Zionist Socialist Party. He was arrested in Rostov-on-Don on December 12, 1925. He was sentenced to expulsion to the Kyrgyz territory for a term of 3 years by a decision of the CCA of the OGPU of January 23, 1926. By decree of the CCA of the OGPU of December 3, 1926, the expulsion was replaced by a trip to Palestine. The decision of the CCA of the OGPU on serving the sentence deprived of the right to reside in Moscow, Leningrad, the North Caucasus, Belarus, Ukraine and Crimea with attachment to a certain place of residence. Settled in Voronezh. He was arrested on August 18, 1930 in case No. 6991. Convicted by a decision of the CCA of the OGPU of December 3, 1930, to imprisonment for 3 years. March 28, 1931-1932 was detained in the Chelyabinsk political prison, in 1933 in the Verkhneuralsk political prison. The further fate is unknown.

[19] GAOPI VO. F. 9353. Op. 2. D.P. - 26427V.1. L.88.

[20] Medushevsky, A.N. Russian Bonapartism as a subject of comparative study // Transactions of the Institute of Russian History. Vol. 5 / Russian Academy of Sciences, Institute of Russian History; open ed. A.N. Sakharov. M .: Nauka, 2005. P. 118-181.

[21] Ovseevich Anatoly Davidovich (1906, the city of Rogachev, Mogilev

province - 1937?). Member of the Zionist Socialist Party. Arrested in Slutsk for belonging to the Jewish Socialist Union of Workers' Youth "Jugend Poalei Zion". Sentenced January 15, 1925 to deportation to the Urals for a term of 3 years. He was serving a link in Irbit. Arrested again. By the decision of the CCA, the OGPU was sentenced to imprisonment for 3 years. He served his sentence in the Tobolsk political prison. In 1927, came under amnesty, the term was reduced. By the decision of the CCA of the OGPU of January 20, 1928, he was deprived of the right to reside in Moscow, Leningrad, Rostov-on-Don, Ukraine and Belarus for 3 years. The city of Voronezh was chosen as the place of settlement. He was arrested on August 18, 1930 in case No. 6991. Condemned by the Resolution of the CCA of the OGPU of December 3, 1930 to imprisonment for 3 years. He was serving his sentence in the Chelyabinsk political prison. By a resolution of the CCA of the OGPU of June 10, 1933, he was released and sent through OGPU to Kazakhstan for a period of 2 years. Included on September 22, 1937 in the Stalinist lists of the Kazakh SSR in the 1st category (execution).

[22] GAOPI VO. F. 9353. Op. 2. D.P. - 26427V.1. L.92

[23] Damier, V.V. Left-wing radical criticism of totalitarianism // Study of dictatorships. The experience of Russia and Germany / Otv. ed. M.B. Korchagin. - M .: Monuments of historical thought, 2007. P.67-75.

[24] Leontyev, Ya. V., Bykovsky, S. M. From the history of the last pages of the anarchist movement in the USSR: the case of A. Baron and S. Ruvinsky (1934) // Petr Alekseevich Kropotkin and the problems of historical and cultural modeling of the development of civilization : Materials of an international scientific conference. St. Petersburg: Solart, 2005.S. 157-171.

[25] Ber Borokhov (June 21 (July 3), 1881, Zolotonosha, Poltava province of the Russian Empire - December 4 (17), 1917, Kiev) is a Jewish politician, ideologist of Zionism, one of the leaders of the Poalei Zion movement.

[26] GAOPI VO. F. 9353. Op. 2. D.P. - 26427V.1. L.122.

[27] Ibid. L.89.

[28] Komissarov Mark Iosifovich (1893, the city of Kerch-?). Member of the Zionist Socialist Party. Arrested in Rostov-on-Don. By a resolution of the OS, the OGPU was sentenced to 3 years in a concentration camp. Upon serving his sentence, by resolution of the OS OGPU of October 7, 1927, he was sentenced to deportation to Siberia. On December 19, 1927, the previous Decree was annulled and by the decision of the CCA of the OGPU of February 17, 1927, after serving his sentence, he was deprived of the right to reside in Moscow, Leningrad, Rostov-on-Don, Ukraine, the Western Territory with an attachment of 3 years. He chose the place of residence in Voronezh. Arrested on August 18, 1930 in case No. 6991. Convicted by a decision of the CCA of the OGPU of December 3, 1930 to be imprisoned in a concentration camp for a term of 3 years. In 1931-1933 he was held in the Chelyabinsk political prison. By resolution of the CCA of the OGPU of June 10, 1933, he was prematurely released and sent to the Northern Territory for 2 years. By the decision of the CCA of the OGPU of November 15, 1934, he was exiled to Bashkiria for the remaining term. The further fate is unknown.

[29] GAOPI VO. F. 9353. Op. 2. D.P. - 26427V.1. L.91.

[30] GAOPI VO. F. 9353. Op. 2. D.P. - 26427V.1. L.91.

[31] Gilodi [Giladi] (Ginzburg) Zoya Borisovna (1908, the city of

Melitopol-?). Member of Gashomer-Gatsair. Arrested in 1926 by the Decree of the CCA of the OGPU of April 29, 1927, was sentenced to deportation to Kazakhstan for a period of 3 years. Upon serving the sentence, by the Decree of the CCA of the OGPU of October 11, 1929, serving the sentence was deprived of the right to reside in Moscow, Leningrad, the North Caucasus, Ukraine, Belarus, and Crimea with attachment to a certain place of residence for 3 years. The city of Voronezh was chosen as the place of settlement. Arrested on August 18, 1930 in case No. 6991. Sentenced by Decree of the CCA of the OGPU of December 3, 1930 to imprisonment in the Urals for 3 years. Arrested on October 24, 1931 in the city of Sverdlovsk and sentenced on February 14, 1932 to 3 years in forced labor camps. She was serving her sentence in the Chelyabinsk politizolator. In November 1934 she was in Verkhneuralsk. According to the decision of the CCA of the OGPU of November 15, 1934, he was exiled to Samarkand for 2 years. Released on November 15, 1936. She chose Samarkand as her place of residence. The further fate is unknown. Husband - Aizik Ilyich Furman.

[32] Lenin, V.I. The collapse of the Second International. Moscow: Moscow Worker, 1924.104 p.

[33] GAOPI VO. F. 9353. Op. 2. D.P. - 26427.V.1. L.91.

[34] Ibid. L.94.

[35] New General Federation of Workers - Histadrut - the main trade union organization of Israel, uniting the majority of country of hired workers of the country.

[36] Ha-Shomer ha-tsagir // Jewish Electronic Encyclopedia. Electronic resource. Access Mode: http://eleven.co.il/zionism/congresses-institutions-parties/11087/.

[37] GAOPI VO. F. 9353. Op. 2. D.P. - 26427.V.1. L.254.

[38] Ibid. L.252

[39] Ibid. L.218

[40] Ibid. L.221

[41] Bauer (Waueg) Otto (1882-1938). One of the leaders of Austrian Social Democracy and the Second International, the ideologist of Austro-Marxism.

[42] Otto Bauer. Das Weltbild des Kapitalismus. Wien, 1924. (German)

[43] A free translation of the title of Fritz Naftali's book, Economic Democracy. Her essence, achievement and goal". See: Fritz Naphtali. Wirtschaftsdemokratie: ihr Wesen, Weg und Ziel. - Berlin: Verlagsges. d. Allgem. Dt. Gewerkschaftsbundes, 1928. (German)

[44] Peretz Naftali (née Fritz Naftali, 1888-1961) - German entrepreneur, journalist, trade union leader; After immigrating to Palestine in 1933, he was a university teacher, financier, and politician in Israel.

[45] Werner Sombart (1863-1941) - German economist, sociologist and historian, philosopher of culture. The author of a number of works on Jewish subjects, which were published in Russia. See: Sombart V. The Future of the Jewish People. Translation by H. I. Greenberg. Odessa: A.M. Printing House Schweitzer, 1912; Sombart V. Jews and economic life. St. Petersburg: Publishing House "Reason", 1912 and others.

[46] Werner Sombart. Die Zukunft des Kapitalismus. Berlin, 1932.

[47] GAOPI VO. F. 9353. Op. 2. D.P. - 26427.V.1. L.254.

[48] GAOPI VO. F. 9353. Op. 2. D.P. - 26427.V.1. L.254.

[49] Ibid. L.133.

[50] Ibid. L.251.

[51] GAOPI VO. F. 9353. Op. 2. D.P. - 26427.V.1. L.255.

[52] Ibid. L.259.

[53] Levit Rosa Osipovna - (1881-1937?) - Bundist since 1902. In 1920, she was a candidate member of the Central Committee of the Bund, then the Secretary of the Bund and the MK of the RSDLP. Arrested for the first time on February 20, 1921, and released on November 28 of the same year. She worked as a secretary of the commission for organizing the Institute of Higher Jewish Knowledge at the People's Commissariat of Education (Institute for the Study of Jewish History, Philology and Literature). Included in the Stalinist lists in the Kazakh SSR 09/22/37 in the 1st category (execution).

[54] Fedorovtsy - a religious movement that arose in the early 1920s in the Voronezh province, one of the "catacomb churches." In November 1929, an open trial took place in Voronezh over the Fedorovites - 36 people were accused of a White Guard conspiracy, anti-Soviet agitation and terrorism. The Voronezh newspaper Kommuna for two weeks printed detailed reports from the process. Numerous rallies of workers were organized in the city, demanding the execution of believers. According to the verdict of the court, 16 people were sentenced to death, the rest were sentenced to various terms of punishment.

[55] GAOPI VO. F. 9353. Op. 2. D.P. - 14667. L. 130.

[56] Ibid. L.131.

[57] Furman Aizik Ilyich (1905, m. Bazaar of the Volyn province -?). Member of Gashomer-Gatsior and the United All-Russian Organization of Zionist Youth (EBOSM). Aresto-van in 1924. OSO OGPU sent to the Urals, escaped from exile. Hiding under the name of Zilberbrand. In 1925, he was arrested in Kiev and imprisoned in the Suzdal prison. In 1927 he was sent to the Yenisei Territory. May 11, 1930 arrived in Voronezh, where he was serving an administrative link. Arrested on March 27, 1932. By a resolution of the CCA of the OGPU of September 23, 1932, he was sentenced to exile in Central Asia for 3 years. He served his sentence in Tashkent. He was released on September 25, 1935. He chose the place of residence in Samarkand. The further fate is unknown. Wife - Gilodi Zoya Borisovna.

[58] Broytman Naum Iosifovich (1911, Odessa-?) Member of Gashomer-Gatsior. Arrested and convicted in 1928 in Odessa. He served a link in Kazakhstan. In 1930 he arrived in Voronezh to serve an administrative link for a period of 3 years. Arrested on April 28, 1932 in the case of the Voronezh organization "Gasmer-Gatsior." By the decision of the CCA of the OGPU of September 23, 1932, he was sent to Siberia. He served a link in Irkutsk. The further fate is unknown.

[59] The Italian strike - a term that came into use of the Russian press in connection with the struggle (in the spring of 1905) Ital. railway workers against government attempts to strip them of the right to strike. The Italian strike (obstruction) is a form of protest along with strike and sabotage, consisting in extremely strict fulfillment by the employees of the enterprise of their duties and rules, not a single step, not departing from them and not a single step, not going beyond them. Sometimes an Italian strike is called Work-to-rule.

[60] GAOPI VO. F. 9353. Op. 2. D.P. - 26331. L.87.

[61] Ibid. L.92.

[62] Genin Boris Peysakhovich (1908, the city of Starodubsk, Chernihiv province -?). Member of the People's Labor (Right) Gehelutz. Arrested in Bryansk and sentenced by the OSO OGPU in 1927 to deportation to Siberia. He served a link in the city of Yeniseisk. In 1930 he arrived in Voronezh to serve an administrative link for a period of 3 years. Arrested on April 28, 1932 in the case of the Voronezh organization Gaschomer-Gatsior. By the decision of the CCA of the OGPU of September 23, 1932, he was sent to Kazakhstan. He was serving a link in Aktyu-Binsk. He was released on July 22, 1935 and remained to live in Aktyubinsk. The further fate is unknown.

[63] Khaimovich Yudif Solomonovna (1905, Odessa -?). Member of the United All-Russian Organization of Zionist Youth (EEWM) since 1922. Arrested in 1924 and sent to the Narym Territory. On the night of December 15-16, 1925, she was arrested in a group case of exiled Zionists (9 people) who created the Narym Zionist Bureau. April 2, 1926 OSO OGPU was sentenced to 3 years in a concentration camp. Due to pregnancy, the political isolator was replaced by a link to the city of Shadrinsk. In 1930, she arrived to serve an administrative exile in Voronezh. On April 27, 1932, she was arrested in the case of the Voronezh organization Gaschomer-Gatsior. By the decision of the CCA of the OGPU of September 23, 1932, he was sent to Western Siberia. It was sent to Novosibirsk, the link was serving in the Minusinsk Territory. Released on May 17, 1935. Further fate is unknown.

[64] Stern Samuel Gershevich (1900, Pinsk, Minsk province -?). Member of the Zionist Socialist Party since 1921, He-holuza since 1924. Arrested on July 11, 1924 in Vinnitsa. Decision of the CCA on December 12, 1924, to the 3rd year of imprisonment in the Solovetsky special purpose camp. On January 31, 1925 he was transferred from Solovki to Kem, and then to the Verkhneuralskiy political isolator. In 1930, he arrived in Voronezh to serve an administrative link. On April 27, 1932, he was arrested in the case of the Voronezh organization Gaschomer-Gatsior. By the resolution of the CCA, the OGPU of September 23, 1932, was sent to Central Asia, sent to Tashkent. He was released early on December 13, 1932, with the right to live freely throughout the USSR. The further fate is unknown.

[65] Bergman Israel Moiseevich (1903, Nikolaev-?) Member of the Zionist Socialist Party. In 1919 he joined the Zionist scout organization. In 1924 he was expelled from the institute and arrested, released on bail. He left the city, hiding in the city of Odessa and the city of Balta under the surnames of others. Arrested in Kiev as Mikhail Brakin. In June–September 1926 he was held in Tagansk prison (Moscow). Sent to Narymsk region for 3 years. In October 1928 he was in Tomsk, in 1929 in Kursk. In March 1932 in exile in Voronezh. By the decree of the CCA of September 23, 1932, he was sent to Kazakhstan. He was serving a link in Aktyubinsk. After his release on July 22, 1935, he remained to live in Aktyubinsk. Arrested on 10/10/1937. Sentenced to 10 years in prison under Art. 58-10. The further fate is unknown.

[66] Popel Solomon Semenovich (1903, Voronezh-?) Member of Gaschomer-Gatsior (?). Accountant plant them. Stalin, Voronezh. Arrested on April 20, 1932 for organizing an Italian strike. By the decision of the CCA of the OGPU of September 23, 1932, he was sent to Kazakhstan. After serving his sentence, he returned to Voronezh. In October 1941, he was drafted into the army and on December 17, 1941, he retired to the front from Voronezh. In March 1942 he went missing.

[67] Akinshin, A. N. The Jewish population in the Voronezh province in the second half of the XIX - early

XX centuries. / A.N. Akinshin // The Population and Territory of the Central Black Earth Region and the West of Russia in the Past and Present: Proceedings of the VII Regional Scientific Conference on Historical Demography and Historical Geography, dedicated to the 75th anniversary of V.P. Zagorovsky (1925-1994), (Voronezh, 20– Apr 21, 2000) / Ed. A.N. Akinshin. Voronezh, 2000. Pp. 43-47.

[68] Nosikov, A. A Brief History of the Voronezh Jewish Community of the 19-20 Century / A. Nosikov // Newsletter of the Interfaith Council at the Voronezh Regional Duma: [collection of articles] / ed. S.A. Well [and others]. - Voronezh, 2017. - No. 8. - Pp. 60-66.

[69] The first general census of the population of the Russian Empire in 1897. Distribution of the population by mother tongue and counties of 50 provinces of European Russia. URL: http: // www.demoscope.ru / weekly / ssp / rus_lan_97_uezd.php? reg = 268

[70] Tidhar D. (Encyclopedia of the pioneers of Yishuv and its builders: images and photographs (Heb.). In 18 vol. T.2 (1947). P. 869.

[71] Belova, I. B. Forced migrants: refugees and prisoners of war of the First World War in Russia. 1914-1925 Moscow: AIRO-XXI, 2014. 431 p.

[72] Zlatina, M.A. Jewish refugees in the Tambov province: problems of building relationships with the local administration, public organizations and the local population (summer 1915). [Text] / M.A. Zlatina // The First World War and the problems of Russian society. materials of the international scientific conference. St. Petersburg, 2014. Pp. 115-119.

[73] Tumanova, A. Jewish public organizations during the First World War (on the example of the Tambov province) // World crisis of 1914-1920 and the fate of East European Jewry. Moscow: ROSSPEN. 2005. Pp. 124-142.

[74] Bakhtin, V.V. Jewish organizations of Voronezh in the first decade of Soviet power [Text] / publ. V.V. Bakhtin // Bityug. - 2017. - No. 2. - Pp. 58-69.

[75] Simonova, Anna Viktorovna. The Zionist movement in Soviet Russia, 1917-1920s: dissertation ... candidate of historical sciences: 07.00.02. Moscow, 1999. 249 p.

[76] Agapov, M.G. The origins of Soviet-Israeli relations: the "Jewish national hearth" in Soviet politics in the 1920s - 1930s: monograph. Tyumen: "Vector Beech", 2011. - 324 p.

[77] Krapivin, M.Yu. The Russian Zionist Organization and the Soviet State in the First Post-Revolutionary Years (1918-1920) [Text] / M.Yu. Krapivin // Russia and the Revolution of 1917: the experience of history and theory: materials of the All-Russian Scientific Conference (St. Petersburg, November 12-13, 2007). SPb., 2008. Pp. 134-149.

[78] Russian Zionism: History and Culture: Proc. conf. / [Editorial. O. Budnitsky et al.]. - M.: House Heb. book. 2002 (OJSC Type. News). 327 p.

[79] Nora Levin, While Messiah Tarried: Jewish Social Movements: 1871-1917 (New York: Schocken Books, 1977).

[80] Jacob Hen-Tov, Communism and Zionism in Palestine During the British Mandate (Cam-bridge, MA: Schenkman Publishing, 1974).

[81] Zvi Gitelman, Century of Ambivalence: The Jews of Russia and the Soviet Union (New York: Schocken Books, 1988); Levin, Jews in the Soviet Union Since 1917: Paradox of Survival, 2 vols. (New York: New York University Press, 1988); Benjamin Pinkus, The Jews of the Soviet Union: The History of

a National Minority (Cambridge, UK: Cambridge University Press, 1988).

[82] Ziva Galili and Boris Morozov, Exiled to Palestine: The Immigration of Zionist Convicts from Soviet Russia, 1924-1934 (London: Routledge, 2006).

[83] Morozov B. Source study of the problem of the expulsion of convicted Zionists from the USSR to Palestine in 1924-1934 // Palestine and Israel from World War II to the present day / Ed. T.A. Karasova, D.A. Maryasis / Institute of Oriental Studies RAS. M.: IV RAS; Publisher Vorobiev A.V., 2016. Pp. 77-119.

Chapter 5

Towards the Development of the Informal Economy: The Case of Street Trading in Ile-Ife, Nigeria

Titilayo Olubunmi Olaposi

Abstract

Previously, scholars in Nigeria have argued for and against the continuing existence of street trading activity in cities but no known study had examined how street trading could be developed. This chapter seeks to provide empirical evidence for its characteristics, values and challenges in order to provide insights into how street traders could be supported to make their trading activity more productive and sustainable. Findings showed that the street traders need entrepreneurship education, financial support and favourable regulatory measures to facilitate the development of their trades. The chapter concludes that street trading could be highly productive and sustainable if adequately supported.

Keywords: challenges, informal economy, street trading, sustainable, values

1. Introduction

Street trading is a type of entrepreneurship that is prevalent in developing countries such as Nigeria. Recently some state governments in Nigeria are taking regulatory measures to prohibit entrepreneurial activities in city streets. However, previous studies have shown that the usual approach of insisting on evicting street vendors has largely been unsuccessful (e.g. with a failure rate of 79.6% in Enugu). Considering that street trading has significant economic values and that damage to it means damage to some UN sustainable development goals, it becomes imperative to seek a policy stand that will foster a win-win situation between city street entrepreneurs and the government. Therefore, the aim of this paper is to provide empirical evidence for the values and challenges of street trading in order to provide insights into how street traders could be supported to make their trading activities sustainable. The objectives of the study therefore are four: (i) to characterise street traders in Ile-Ife city; (ii) to examine the economic, health and other impacts of street trading; (iii) to investigate the challenges of street trading; and (iv) to develop strategies for sustainable street trading in cities.

1.1 Background

The role of entrepreneurship in national economic development cannot be over emphasised. Entrepreneurship has contributed to the economic growth of most advanced countries tremendously; especially, in the areas of overall employment generation and gross domestic product (GDP) [1, 2]. Small businesses are now recognised to be indispensable in economic development. They are the driving force of economic growth, job creation, and poverty reduction; especially in developing countries. Through small businesses, accelerated economic growth and rapid industrialisation have been achieved [2]. In Nigeria, the potential contribution of small businesses to employment and income has been greatly appreciated.

The development of small and medium enterprises requires governmental support. In recognition of this, many nations of the world have instituted enterprise support networks and structures to enhance their development. In Nigeria, since the 1970s, the government has designed and introduced measures to promote small-and medium-enterprise development [3]. These measures have included fiscal, monetary and export incentives. For example, the Central Bank of Nigeria (CBN) has established provisions for loans for small businesses through commercial and merchant banks. Several developmental financial institutions and schemes were established to aid small businesses. The agencies mandated for this include the Nigerian Bank of Commerce and Industry (NCBI), the Nigerian Industrial Development Bank (NIDB), and the World Bank SME I and SME II initiatives. Further, export incentives are established by the Nigerian Export–Import Bank (NEXIM). This makes possible the stimulation of export loan facilities given to small businesses. Also, export duty exemptions are administered by the Nigeria Export Promotion Council (NEPC). Further, the establishment of research institutes and technology incubation centres (TICs), the Small and Medium Enterprises Development Agency of Nigeria (SMEDAN), National Directorate for Employment (NDE) including the promulgation of the Nigerian Enterprises Promotion Decree (NEPD) of 1972 which was revised in 1977, are some of the means through which the Nigerian government has encouraged entrepreneurship development in the country [4, 5]. Other small business incentive programmes such as personnel training, repair and maintenance of specialised machines, and extension services are part of the support services made available to Nigerian small and medium enterprises. Aside the efforts of the Federal Government of Nigeria, state and local governments also have established some small-business assistance programmes. All these support efforts are laudable and are needed by the SMEs but there is a group of traders who also operate microbusinesses that are of value to mankind but that are not provided for in all the support initiatives. These are street traders.

The problem of unemployment of youths has generated an informal type of trading called street trading. In urban settings in many developing countries, due to migration and industrialisation, street trading has formed an integral part of the informal sector. In many cities, street trading has become a source of livelihood for many and also, has become an important source of accessible, convenient and affordable goods for the urban poor. For example, the street food sector provides accessible food items and makes life easy for the working class. Beyond this, the socio-economic role of street trading in terms of its potential for employment and income generation has attracted many people, both male and female, single and married, into the practice. Although some people see and react to street traders as a nuisance, the forces that created their market have made them an inextricable part of the social fabric.

Street trading is currently prevalent in Nigeria. Selling items from a vehicle, a cart or a make-shift shop on a public street is allowed in the cities without a permit. Male and female traders placing their wares on their head, hand or shoulder hawking on streets or displaying their wares in front of residential buildings or in make shift shops are commonly found in Nigerian cities. Such traders take opportunities of heavy traffic and the consequent frequent hold-ups to sell their goods to drivers and passengers inside vehicles. Other of such traders display their wares in public sidewalks. Street traders may stay in the business for many years, not planning to change to any other form of business; but some may do it for some time and quit when they get a salaried job or when they are able to afford better forms of businesses.

Very recently, some state governments became worried about street traders cluttering the walkways in the capital cities, littering the area with trash and creating unfair competition for shop owners; and so, made moves to ban street trading in the cities. For example, Lagos State government, in 2016 banned buying and selling in streets. Defaulters (both buyers and sellers) would be fined. They would either pay N90,000 or serve a six-month jail term. This was said to be done in line with the Lagos State Street Trading and Illegal Markets Prohibition Law, 2003 which restricted street trading and hawking in the metropolis. Sections seven and eight of the law gave jurisdiction and power to the Special Court to order the seizure and public auction of items impounded from street traders and Section 10 of the law prescribes a N5,000 fine or three months imprisonment upon conviction. This law, for a period of about thirteen years, was not enforced until 2016 when the state government became disturbed about the unregulated activities of street traders in the city of Lagos. The government's action received reactions from both traders and buyers who were very displeased.

Evidence from previous empirical studies have suggested that the disadvantages of street trading indeed outweigh the advantages [6]. Therefore, it may seem justifiable to outlaw the practice. However, when street traders are not allowed to practice their trade and are not supported to operate any better business, they go back to joblessness which culminates in hunger and poverty. Thus, infringing on Sustainable Development Goals (SDGs) 1 and 2 (to end poverty and eradicate hunger).

This paper argues that street traders should not be sent out of business, rather they should be supported to transform their businesses to more sustainable forms. If adequately supported, street trading could be transformed into more productive sustainable technological or non-technological SMEs. This paper, based on empirical evidence, addresses four questions: (i) What are the characteristics of street traders in Ile-Ife city? (ii) What are the economic, health and other impacts of street trading? (iii) What are the challenges of street trading? and (iv) What kind of support do street traders need to make their businesses more productive and sustainable?

2. Literature review

Street trading is a phenomenon that has attracted the attention of researchers for some time. Scholars from different disciplines have taken the issue in different directions. Some have argued in its favour, while some have argued against it. In favour of street trading, Brinkley et al. [7] submitted that "small, mobile retailers such as produce trucks and healthy street food vendors may offer better food environment interventions because they require little start-up, can easily target schools and neighbourhoods with poor access to healthful foods, and circumvent the need to own real estate." Their study demonstrated that kerbside produce vendors successfully supply a range of whole fruits and vegetables in a predominantly low- and middle-income African American section of Philadelphia at prices lower than conventional food outlets. Moreover, they argued that "because the majority of produce trucks have operated as stable and profitable businesses for decades and survived where neighbourhood supermarkets have closed, they may present a viable long-term solution for providing low-income neighbourhoods with fresh produce."

Street trading as a source of income and as a source of employment opportunity is established by previous authors [8]. Anetor [8] reported that the reasons for involving in street hawking include inability to secure formal jobs, constraints (including finance) in gaining admission to higher school and joblessness of the family's breadwinners. Therefore, street trading provides them a means of sourcing income for the traders and their family members. The value of street trading has been established in the literature. For example, street food industry has been found to play an important role in supplying the food requirements of an urban population [9] and street food has been found to serve a very high percentage of travellers, industrial workers and school children. On one hand, street trading is a source of self-employment to poor men and women and on the other hand, it serves as a means of providing low-cost, as well as 'convenient' services to a majority of the urban population. Inolia [10] reported that street trading had contributed immensely to the social and economic life of Nigerians.

On the contrary, Amegah and Jaakkola [11] argued that street trading is hazardous to the health of the traders and is a substandard form of employment. Therefore, they recommended that street trading be eliminated from economically developing countries. Amoo et al. [12] assessed the health risks associated with street trading activities among selected mothers in urban centres of Nigeria and concluded that street trading is a risky type of business activity that makes women to be more vulnerable to workplace hazards. Also, Olurinola et al. [13] reported that the activities of street traders are associated with a number of health hazards. This is corroborated by the submission of Adedeji et al. [14] who examined the spatial implication of street trading in Osogbo, Nigeria. They found that street trading activity has serious negative impacts on accessibility, generated erection of illegal structures, solid waste, traffic congestion, auto-accident, and deface of urban aesthetics. Also, in support of the foregoing, Taiwo and Akinyode [6] submitted that street trading contributes to vehicular and pedestrian congestion that cause traffic accident, increase pollution and impede the flow of police, ambulance, and other emergency vehicles. He also asserted that street trading often results in the blockage of the routes of egress from crowded building such as theatres and stadia thus, increasing the scale of tragedy in the event of a major fire, explosion, or toxic gas escape. The author further submitted that street food vendors pose major public health problems because they often expose their goods to the sun, air pollution and contamination by passers-by.

Also, the issue of children hawkers has been used to argue that street trading has negative impact on even the under age. Ashimolowo et al. [15] studied the effect of child street trading activities and found that street trading has negative effects on children. Further, it was noted that there is a high tendency for the girl child to forgo her education and thereby lose all the benefits of education. Another group of researchers, Ojo and Olufemi [16] investigated the effects of child street hawking in Nigeria. They found that parents' levels of education, parents' occupations and the sizes of the family were significantly related to the problem of child hawkers in the study area. Clark and Yesufu [17] also carried out an investigation on the issue of child street trading. The results of their study showed that a greater proportion of the child street traders combined work with schooling. Whereas, in their own study, Ugochukwu et al. [18] found a contradictory result. They found that the parents of all child street traders were of low socio-economic status and that trading was taking place during school hours for financial gains of the family.

All the researchers who condemned street trading based on its negative effects failed to establish how street traders could be supported so as to improve their businesses and reduce or totally eliminate the inherent risks. Their criticism of the trading activity is only capable of sending the traders out of business and turning them into poverty and hunger. This leaves a gap in the extant literature which this paper seeks to fill.

2.1 Theoretical background

Entrepreneurship consists of leading in creation of a new business to produce and deliver something innovative, in the view of customers to the marketplace. Entrepreneurship is the process of generating something new by allocating the compulsory time and exertion, and expect to receive rewards of monetary and individual satisfaction and freedom [19].

Businesses are categorised by means of their sizes as micro, small, medium and large. Also, it is common knowledge that businesses could develop from one scale to another. For example, a micro business could grow to become a small business. Micro, small and medium enterprises (MSMEs) exist and evolve in economic systems performing active roles in reducing poverty, economic empowerment and growth [20]. The definition of micro enterprise has been expanded to include those who engage in small-scale vending, services, repair and enterprise activities [21].

2.2 What is street trading?

Street trading is a common phenomenon and an integral component of urban economies in many countries of the world. It has existed for hundreds of years and is considered as a cornerstone of many cities' historical and cultural heritage [22]. Street trading is also referred to as street vending, hawking or street entrepreneurship. It involves selling or offering for sale any article in any street (including all forecourts, roads, footways and other areas next to streets) or open space where the public have access without payment [23]. Street trading has been defined in many ways. According to Amoah-Mensah [24], street hawkers or vendors are sellers without permanent structures. Some street traders sell products while some provide services. From street trading came the concept of 'street food.' According to FAO [25], "Street foods are ready-to-eat foods and beverages prepared and/or sold by vendors or hawkers especially in the streets and other similar places." Some street traders are mobile, carrying their wares on their heads in pans or trays. Some hold their wares in their hands or bags; while some put their wares in wheel barrows or carts pulled by the sellers. Another group of street traders are stationary; they sell their products or provide their services in a location.

2.3 Street trading activity and the informal economy

More than 60 per cent of the world's employed population earn their livelihoods in the informal economy. Informality exists in all countries regardless of the level of socio-economic development although it is more prevalent in developing countries [26]. The term *informality* means different things to different people. It is often thought of in terms of things like unprotected workers, low productivity, unfair competition, evasion of the rule of law, underpayment or non-payment of taxes, and work "underground" or in the shadows. The informal economy refers to workers and enterprises that operate informally [27]. The ILO [28] indicates that informal employment includes agricultural day labourers and urban street vendors. In the informal economy, more women than men, youths and older people as well as less-educated workers are involved [27].

The informal employment is classified into two: Self-employment in informal enterprises, comprising employer/owner operators, own-account workers, and unpaid contributing family member and wage-employment in formal jobs, comprising employees of informal enterprises, casual day labourers, domestic workers, and industrial outworkers [29].

The general features that are associated with the informal sector include the following: (i) Lack of legal protection for workers concerning labour and social services, (ii) Limited access to formal/regulated markets and subsidies, (iii) High interest rates for loans leading to high capital costs, (iv) Personal and business properties are usually not separated, (v) Organisation based on family, ethnic and/or religious relationships (vi) Contracts are not written, (vii) Dominated by women

(viii) Children are also employed, and (ix) Earnings are consumed directly therefore nothing is left for reinvestment [30].

The demerits of the informal sector have been established in the extant literature. According to ILO [31], policy-makers, workers' and employers' organisations and academics increasingly acknowledge that the high incidence of informality in all its aspects is a major challenge for sustainable development. According to the report, Informality has a harmful effect on workers' rights, including fundamental principles and rights at work, social protection, decent working conditions and the rule of law. It also has a negative impact on the development of sustainable enterprises (especially in terms of low productivity and lack of access to finance), public revenues and governments' scope of action, particularly with regard to economic, social and environmental policies, the robustness of institutions, and fair competition in national and international markets.

Street trading has been frequently associated with informality. For example, in the City of Johannesburg, the term *informal* is used as a synonym of street trading [32]. However, Bénit-Gbaffou has argued that street trading is not automatically informal [32]. According to him, the notion that every street trade is informal is derived from the classic definition by Castells and Portes [33] which states that informal activities refer to ways of income generation that are 'unregulated by the institutions of society, in a legal and social environment in which similar activities are regulated'. Bénit-Gbaffou explained that the notion of formality and informality is essentially linked to management and by-laws and how they are defined. It is the by-laws that define the boundaries of formality and informality and they often shift. Therefore, he asserted that street trading could be formal or informal. The argument of Bénit-Gbaffou is substantiated by the fact that street trading has been formalised, legalised and well managed in some countries (for example, the United States of America) and is therefore no longer informal (i.e. breaking the law).

2.4 Theories of street entrepreneurship

To explain the concept of street entrepreneurship in emerging market economies, four competing theories have emerged [34]. These include: (i) the modernisation perspective which holds that such endeavour is a pre-modern traditional activity; (ii) the structuralist perspective that describes such activity as necessity-driven; (iii) the neo-liberal perspective depicting such endeavour as a rational economic choice; and (iv) the post-modern perspective portraying such activity as voluntarily pursued but more by social actors for cultural reasons. Below, each is reviewed in turn.

2.4.1 Modernisation perspective: a pre-modern traditional economic activity

The modernisation perspective views and assumed that street hawkers and peddlers are a residue from an earlier pre-modern era and their persistence taken as a signal of 'under-development', 'traditionalism' and 'backwardness'. Meanwhile, emergent modern formal economy, was seen to represent 'progress', 'development' and 'advancement'. In this view, street vendors are depicted as 'a residual labour category' which some view as 'unimportant' and 'destined to disappear' [34].

From this perspective, the future is viewed in terms of modern shopping centres, supermarkets and department stores; while street entrepreneurs are seen as either parasitic or inefficient. In this view, street trading is described as 'a disorderly and superfluous activity that cluttered the urban environment, interrupted traffic flows, and competed unfairly with new, large, hygienic commercial establishments. Therefore, according to this perspective, it is something to be eradicated [35].

2.4.2 Structuralist perspective: a necessity-driven activity

The structuralist perspective depicts street trading as a survival practice conducted out of economic necessity as a last resort in the absence of alternative means of livelihood [36]. In this view, such entrepreneurship is a direct by-product of the advent of a de-regulated open world economy. Based on this view, street entrepreneurs are depicted as unwilling and unfortunate pawns in an exploitative global economic system. Therefore, for such marginalised populations, street trading 'is the only means for survival'. Street trading activities are depicted by structuralist perspective as necessity-driven endeavour which is highly insecure and unstable, composed of long hours, poor conditions, no legal or social protection, limited access to credit and very limited bargaining power.

2.4.3 Neo-liberal perspective: a rational economic choice

From the neo-liberal perspective, street entrepreneurship is more a matter of choice than due to a lack of choice. For these neo-liberals, such entrepreneurs are heroes throwing off the shackles of a burdensome state and making a rational economic decision to enter street trading so as to escape over-regulation in the formal realm. Therefore, street entrepreneurship is viewed as the people's 'spontaneous and impoverished masses.' It is a rational economic strategy pursued by entrepreneurs whose spirit is stifled by state-imposed institutional constraints and who voluntarily operate in the informal economy to avoid the costs, time and effort of formal registration.

2.4.4 Post-modern perspective: entrepreneurs as cultural/social actors

The fourth perspective, the post-modern perspective, depicts street entrepreneurship as voluntarily chosen but not a rational economic decision. It is seen more as a cultural endeavour. Thus, street entrepreneurs are viewed more as social actors. The focus of this view is on how the social relations between street entrepreneurs differ to normal market relations in that business and friendship relations blur and there is greater community solidarity and reciprocity, and also, on how exchange relations between street entrepreneurs and their customers differ to mainstream market relations in that without recourse to a legal contract, interpersonal relations and trust become more important [37]. Moreover, there has been a focus on how such entrepreneurship is pursued as a choice because of the greater personal freedom and flexibility it affords and allows them to gain control over their lives e.g., [42]. Another point of focus in this view is how street trading is often in the eyes of participants an expression of community support which allows customers to source goods they otherwise could not afford [38].

3. Research methods

The study was carried out in Ile-Ife, an ancient Yoruba city in Southwestern Nigeria. Ile Ife is said to be dated back around 500 B.C. when it was founded and is the oldest Yoruba city. The city is located in present day Osun State. Geographically, Ile- Ife lies within longitudes 4° 36′E and 4° 56′E and latitudes 7° 28′ N and 7° 46′ N. It is about 218 kilometres northeast of Lagos. To her west lies Ibadan and to the east lies Akure, gateway to the major Yoruba towns. It is about 40 km to Osogbo, the capital of Osun State. Evidence of the urbanisation of Ile-Ife dates back to around 500 AD. Today, it is one of the prominent towns of the State [39].

Ile-Ife is a home to two universities (one private and one federal) and a private polytechnic; as well as a federal government-owned teaching hospital. Administratively, Ile-Ife has two local governments namely Ife Central and Ife East with a population of 167, 254 and 188, 027 inhabitants in 2006 respectively [40].

Data was generated for this paper from a set of primary data gathered among street traders in Ile-Ife. Interview guide was used to elicit information from traders who gave oral informed consent to participate in the study. Sixty (60) participants were selected using stratified random sampling technique. The interview questions were directed towards generating information to characterise the street traders and to understand the gains and pains of the activity so as to be able to determine the support needs of the traders.

The questions for the interview sessions captured (i) socio-demographic characteristics of the respondents (gender, age, parental background, highest educational qualification, previous entrepreneurship education experience, marital status, number of children and dependants and length of street trading experience); (ii) the characteristics of street trades [nature of business e.g. food selling, clothes selling etc.; category of street trading (e.g. mobile, stationary); pre-street trading employment status; and economic gains of the business]; (iii) achievement issues (achievements since the trader engaged in street trading e.g. buy land, build a personal house, sponsoring child(ren)'s education etc.); (iv) traders' perception of and satisfaction with street trading; (v) health and other hazards associated with street trading; (vi) growth plan of the traders for their venture; and (vii) interaction with the government.

4. Results and discussion

4.1 The characteristics of the street traders

Most of the traders were female (80.0%) while just 20.0% were male (**Figure 1**).

About 62.0% were youths (less than 40 years of age) and the rest 38.0% were above 40 years (**Figure 2**).

The highest percentage of the traders (70.0%) had secondary school qualification, about 27.0% did not go beyond primary school but 3.3% attended tertiary institutions of learning (**Figure 3**).

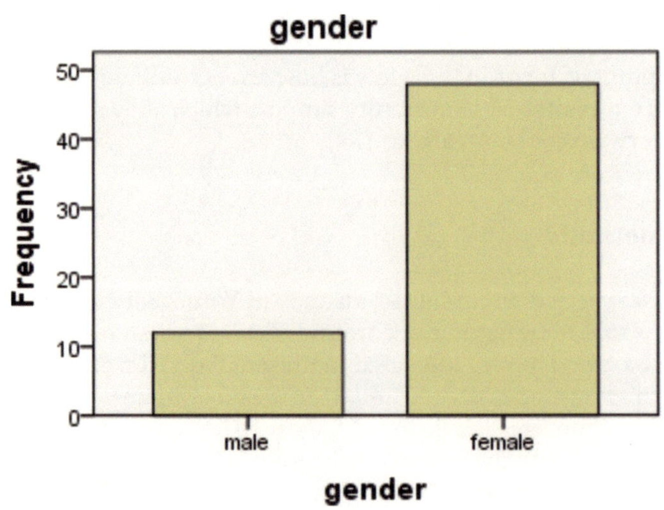

Figure 1.
Respondents' gender.

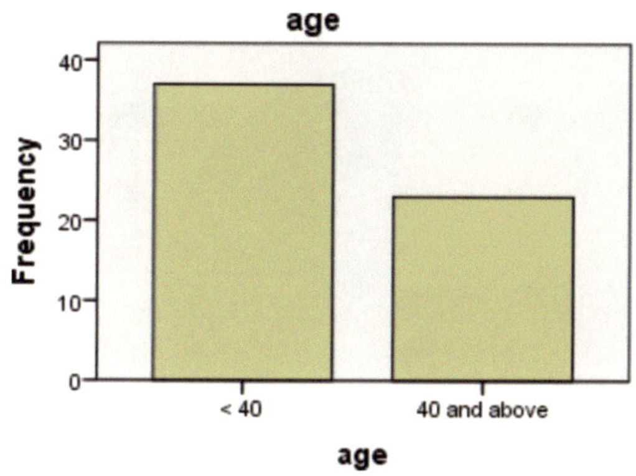

Figure 2.
Respondents' age.

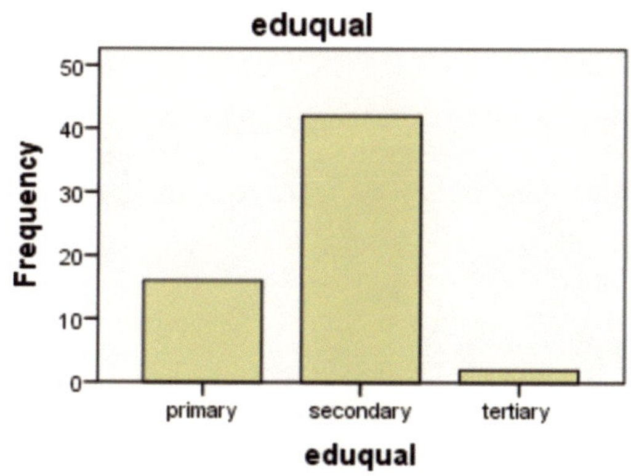

Figure 3.
Respondents' highest educational qualification.

Some (32%) of the traders were single, 65% were married and 3.3% were widows (**Figure 4**).

Some 35.0% of the traders did not have any child but some 46.6%% had either 3 or 4 children (23.3% each) (**Figure 5**).

While 70.0% of the traders did not indicate that they had any dependant, some 20.0% reported that each of them had one dependant and the remaining 10.0% claimed that they had 2 dependants each (**Figure 6**).

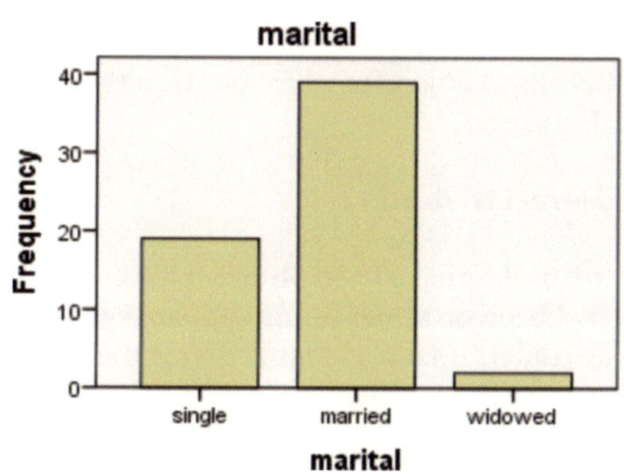

Figure 4.
Respondents' marital status.

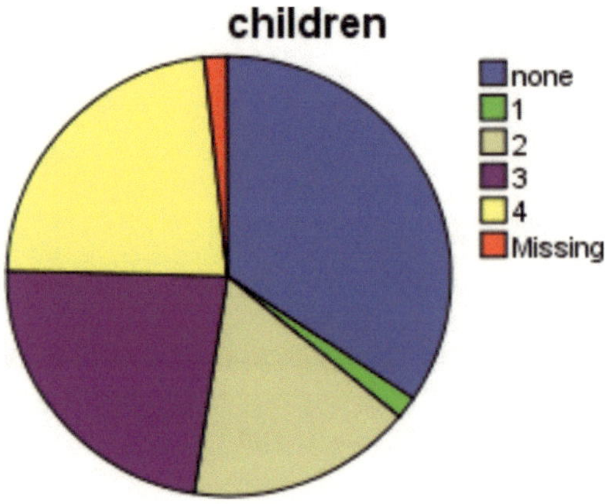

Figure 5.
Respondents' number of children.

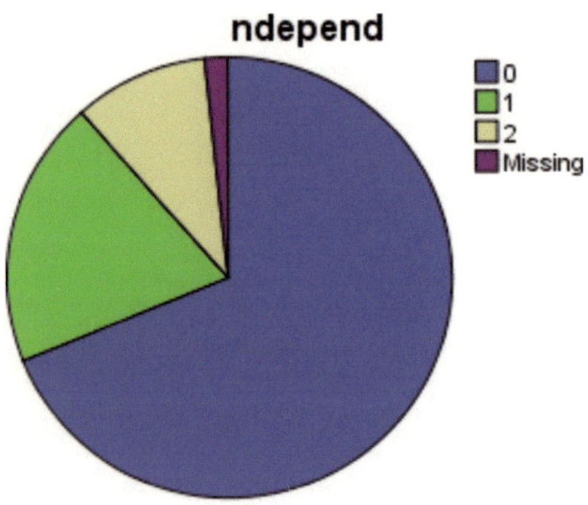

Figure 6.
Respondents' number of dependants.

Most (73.8%) of the fathers were self-employed, 11.5% were unemployed, just 13.1% worked for established organisations and received monthly salaries (**Figure** 7).

Most (73.8%) of the mothers of the respondents were self-employed, 16.4% were unemployed while 8.2% worked to earn salaries in established organisations (**Figure 8**).

Most of the traders had poor parents. Most of the parents (93.4%) were claimed to belong to lower social class while just 3,9% were said to belong to middle class. The remaining 1.6% refused to mention the social class their parents belonged to (**Figure 9**).

4.2 Characteristics of street trades

Many (65.0%) of the traders have been on street for between 1 and 5 years while the remaining 35.0% had been on street for more than 5 years.

Most (62.3%) of the traders operated mobile street trade while 36.1% operated on the stationary category (**Figure 10**).

Most (88.0%) of the traders was never employed while the rest (12%) were previously employed but started street trading when they lost their jobs (**Figure 11**).

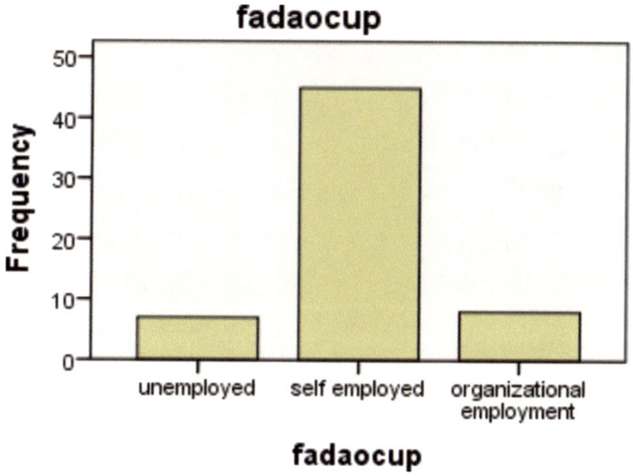

Figure 7.
Categories of respondents' fathers' occupation.

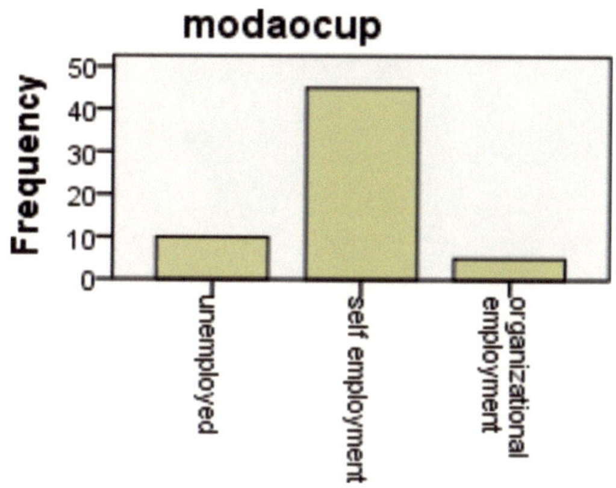

Figure 8.
Categories of respondents' mothers' occupation.

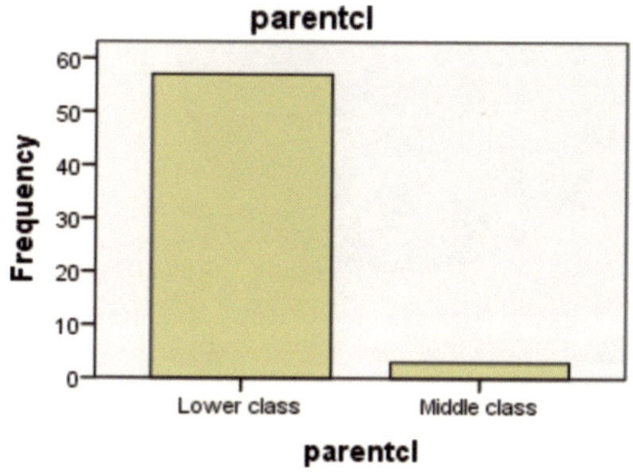

Figure 9.
Respondents' parents social class.

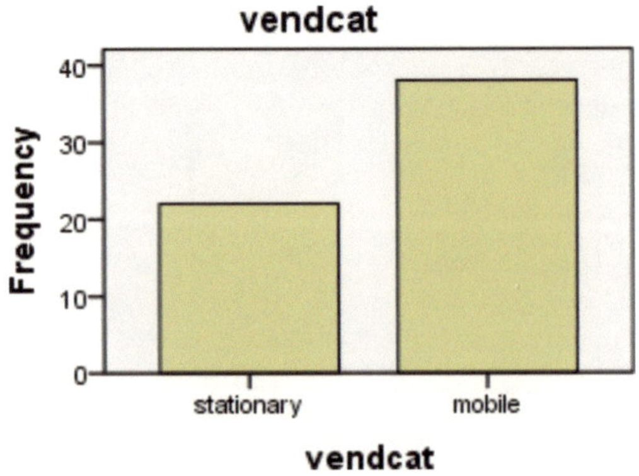

Figure 10.
Respondents' vending categories.

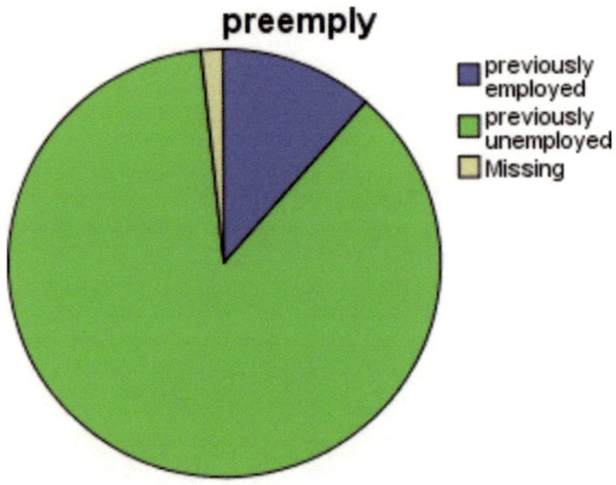

Figure 11.
Respondents' employment history.

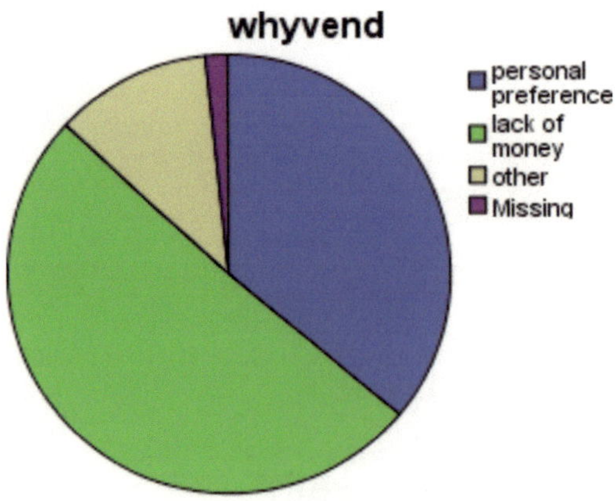

Figure 12.
Respondents' reasons for vending.

Their reasons for street trading include mostly personal preference (36%) and lack of capital (51%). The Figure shows that lack of money takes about half of the space and this makes it outstandingly important (**Figure 12**).

This study shows that street trading generates more profit than the salaries earned by some paid workers in Nigeria. Most (80.0%) of the traders made a profit of between 1000 Naira (about US$3) and 2000 Naira (about US$ 6) per day. Very few of the traders (8.3%) reported that they had less than five hundred Naira as daily profit. Some 11.7% had between five hundred Naira and one thousand Naira. However, most (98.3%) of the traders could not save more than 500 Naira per day due to their financial commitments and obligations (**Figure 13**).

4.3 Achievements of street traders

Only about 7.0% of the traders reported that they had not achieved anything beyond feeding since they started street trading but the rest 93.0% reported they had achieved some things with their trade. About 38.0% perceived the level of their achievements as low, 40.0% as average, 11.7% as high while 3.3% reported that they had very high level of achievements. Some 20.0% had built houses in which they lived from the proceeds of the trade (**Figure 14**).

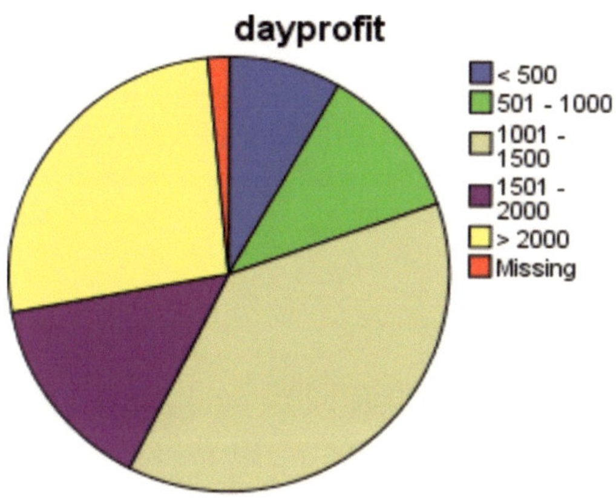

Figure 13.
Respondents' daily profit.

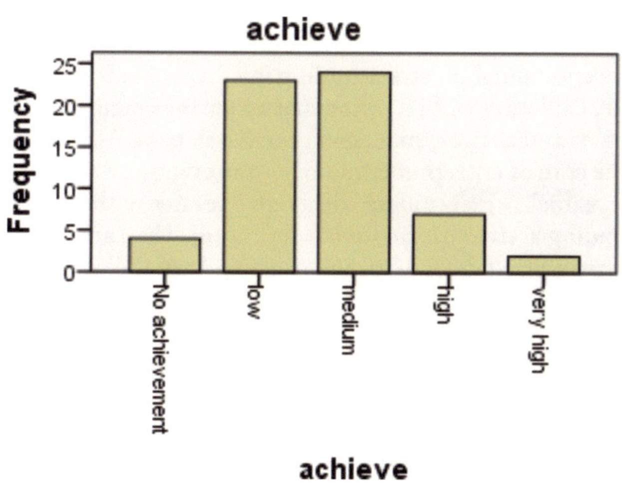

Figure 14.
Respondents' achievements with street trading proceeds.

4.4 Traders' perception of and satisfaction with street trading

Most (72.0%) of the traders perceived street trading as yielding more income than some formal businesses. However, some 13.3% acknowledged that street trading is associated with risks. Only 13.4% reported that they were dissatisfied with street trading. The rest were either neutral or claimed to be satisfied. Most (97%) of the traders believed that street trading yielded more revenue than similar formal businesses.

4.5 Health and other hazards associated with street trading

Some health challenges were found to be associated with street trading. The ailments reported by the selected traders include headache (28.0%), body pain (47.0%) and malaria (25.0%). However, most (72.0%) of the traders perceived the health effects of street trading as not too serious. Only 13.3% had experienced motor accident and only 1.7% has experienced street fight.

4.6 Plan for venture growth

About half of the street traders have some plan for future growth for their ventures, the other half do not have any plan, they seemed to be okay with the present form of their business. Even those that claimed to have plan, the plans seemed to be like wishes because they were not doing anything specifically to show that they were planning for growth.

4.7 Interaction with government

The street traders (100.0%) reported very minimal interaction with the government. The only activity that connects them with the government is the payment of a certain amount of money, a form of daily tax which they referred to as ticket.

5. Discussion

Street trading appears to be the first rung on the entrepreneurial ladder and so could be harnessed for sustainable entrepreneurship development. Based on some definitions of entrepreneurship, street trading is a form of recognised entrepreneurship. For example, Collins et al. [41] opine that an entrepreneur is someone who independently owns and actively manages a small business. Also, Timmons [42] asserts that "At the core of entrepreneurship lies the creation of new business ventures by individuals or teams". Street traders, although operates with very small quantity of goods, their trading activity fits in to this definition. They are independent, doing business and are generating income for themselves. Also, the definition of small and medium businesses (SMEs) has been expanded to include micro businesses and so the emergence of a new concept MSMEs which means micro, small and medium enterprises. From the definition of the National Council of Industry for MSMEs, the definition of Micro Enterprise was interpreted to mean "any enterprise employing between one to nine people and having a capital base from one Naira to five million Naira excluding cost of land." [43]. By this standard, the definition of micro businesses embraces street trading. This is an indication of the acceptance and importance of street trading in an economy. More so that it has been said that.

Micro, small and medium scale enterprises (MSMEs) is accepted globally as a tool for empowering the citizenry and economic growth. They are recognised to be vital in the development of developing economies like Nigeria for reasons such as income generation, social and political role in local employment creation, balanced resources utilisation, utilisation of local technology and raw materials in helping to promote change in a gradual and peaceful manner [44].

Also, with the overall objective of reducing poverty through wealth and job creation and facilitating national economic development, the micro, small and medium enterprises are perceived as the oil required to lubricate the engine of socio-economic transformation [44]. Based on the foregoing, it is clear that while street trading might be encumbered with challenges, it could serve as a means to an end. Therefore, it will not be the best decision to rubbish, castigate and destroy it. The entrepreneurial energies of small businesses like street traders should not be imperilled by subjecting them to discrimination, frustration and persecution. It would be more beneficial to look for ways to support the street traders, to enable them resolve their challenges and thereby, improve their method of trading. This study shows that many of the traders have been operating in streets for more than five years. The entrepreneurial experience they have gathered could be a good leverage for better forms of businesses if they were adequately supported. Moreover, this study shows that most of the traders had never been formally employed. Therefore, street trading is their only hope of gaining livelihood in a responsible manner.

From this paper, it is obvious that in the study area, youths are more involved in street trading than elderly people. Therefore, any support given to street traders would be an activity supporting poor youths to reduce hunger and poverty. This in turn, might reduce the rate of crime in the society. Street traders are hard-working Nigerians just trying to make an honest living, if they are rendered jobless, they may go into crime.

Also, from **Table 1**, it is clear that most of the traders are married with children and some even have dependants. If they are sent out of business, the traders, their children and dependants will suffer and this may turn around to affect the society negatively. Such victims of the circumstance may turn to become beggars in streets, or disturbing the peace of the community.

The study shows that most of the traders operate the mobile form of street vending. This form of street trading is likely to be as hazardous to the health of the street traders. This justifies some governments' negative disposition towards street trading. However, learning from countries such as the United States of America, India and others, provision of space for street traders to erect shops not a long distance to the road will reduce hawking in traffics and will be of benefit to the traders as well as the people patronising them.

This study reveals that most of the street traders have limited level of education. This gives insight into the reason why they could not engage in better forms of employment than street trading. Also, it was found that the street traders lacked entrepreneurship education/training. This confirms the assertion of Amegah and Jaakkola [11] that the urban poor are mostly uneducated or have low educational attainment. Education is a powerful tool in any poverty alleviation programme. It is a means to provide individuals with the requisite knowledge and skills to improve their livelihoods. Nigerian governments at the three tiers (federal, state and local) should therefore extend access to entrepreneurship education to those who already are practising entrepreneurship in streets. Therefore, to support them to improve their businesses and make them more sustainable, there is need to develop suitable programmes for them to enable them acquire entrepreneurial and managerial education. Attendance at such programmes has to be free of cost because, it has been shown that the traders as well as their parents are poor.

Another important need of the traders is capital. It is common knowledge that any meaningful business requires capital. However, micro enterprises tend to lack capital to start or even expand their business, and this has affected the level of

Characteristics	Frequency	Percentage
Gender		
Male	12	20.0
Female	48	80.0
Total	60	100.0
Age		
<40	37	61.7
40 and above	23	38.3
Total	60	100.0
Marital Status		
Single	19	31.7
Married	39	65.0
Widowed	02	03.3
Total	60	100.0
Highest Educational Qualification		
Primary	16	26.7
Secondary	42	70.0
Tertiary	02	03.3
Total	60	100.0
Length of Trading Experience		
1–5 years	39	65.0%
>5 years	21	35.0%
Total	60	100.0%
Number of Children		
0	21	35.0
1	01	1.7
2	10	16.7
3	14	23.3
Total	60	100.0
Traders' Parents' Occupation		
Mother's Occupation	Frequency	Percentage
Unemployed	07	11.7
Self-employed	45	75.0
Salaried employment	08	13.3
Total	60	100.0
Father's Occupation		
Unemployed	10	16.7
Self-employed	45	75.0
Salaried employment	05	08.3
Total	60	100.0
Respondents' parents' social class		
Lower Class	57	95.0
Middle class	03	05.0
Total	60	100.0

Characteristics	Frequency	Percentage
Number of Dependants		
0	42	70.0
1	12	20.0
2	06	10.0
Total	60	100.0

Table 1.
Socio-demographic characteristics of street traders.

Achievement	Frequency	Percentage
Traders' Residence Category		
Parent's house	12	20
Rented house	30	50
Living with a friend	06	10
Personal house	12	20
Total	60	100
Traders' Perception of Level of Achievement		
No achievement	04	06.7
Low	23	38.3
Medium	24	40.0
High	07	11.7
Very high	02	03.3
Total	60	100.0

Table 2.
Achievements of street traders.

success of a lot of such enterprises in Nigeria. To start micro enterprises, entrepreneurs tend to depend upon their personal or family savings. Such is the case of the street traders whose family members are poor and hence, could not support them. Further, this study shows that the daily savings of a large proportion of them were very small, below five hundred Naira. This could never be sufficient to be relied upon for business development and growth, knowing full well that other commitments and obligations will take away part of the savings from time to time. Obviously, there is a need for external support. The matter is worse because most of them cannot meet the requirements for commercial loans from banks [45].

Table 2 shows that some of the traders have gotten some levels of achievement. Some claimed they sponsor their children in school and some, even though not many, claimed they had built houses of their own. This means that, if supported, street trading could be a meaningful and sustainable source of livelihood to some people. This supports Inolia's [10] assertion that street trading had contributed immensely to the social and economic life of Nigerians.

Actually, most of the street traders believed that "street trading yields more income than some formal trades." This may explain why about 88.0% did not feel dissatisfied with street trading. This is corroborated by the notion that street trading is a source of income and employment opportunity [12].

In support of Olurinola et al.'s [13] report that the activities of street traders are associated with a number of health hazards, this study shows that street trading is challenged by some health and other hazards. However, most of the traders did not consider the hazards and health issues to be too serious for them to cope with. This may be because they consider ability to generate income to be of more weight than the health problems they might have.

Lastly, this study reveals that some of the traders were thinking of growth. This is an indication that any effort to assist the growth of their businesses would be embraced. It is clear from this study that government at any level, did not have the street traders in their plan. They collected daily levy from them but did not include them in national development and are not positively regulated. This indeed is unfortunate because it shows that the importance of the activities of the street traders to the economy was not appreciated.

6. Conclusion

Street trading has benefits to traders and others. The major needs identified from this study were capital and entrepreneurship education/training. Most of the respondents had poor parents that could not support them with funds for entrepreneurship development. Also, they had low level of education and no formal entrepreneurship education. Thus, they were not trained for enterprise development.

Four points are established in this paper: First, the value of street trading in poverty alleviation has to be publicly recognised and appreciated. Second, the activity has to be officially regulated in favour of the traders and the community as a whole. Third, street traders need to be supported by giving free entrepreneurship education to the traders. This will enable them to grow and expand their businesses. When this occurs, more benefits will be derived from the businesses. More people may be employed and poverty may thereby be completely eradicated. Fourth, supporting street traders with capital will go a long way to improve on the nature of their trading activity. This may make them more responsible and make their businesses more valuable to their communities and to the nation as a whole.

Based on these findings, we offer some policy recommendations. Though they are context-specific to Ile-Ife, we believe that the model, and thus the recommendations, may hold relevance beyond the current study area.

6.1 Policy recommendations

1. Street and informal traders require laws that recognise their economic activities as an important component of the urban economy, and ensure their right to trading space.

2. Street trading is a means of livelihood for some people and therefore, should be considered for inclusive physical planning for economic sustainability of the urban poor. Policy measures that incorporate design of trading space for the street traders may be of assistance to solve the problems of street trading activities.

3. Street traders are to be involved in the plan for youth entrepreneurship education.

4. Organised street traders are to be included in loan schemes which are directed towards supporting small businesses.

Author details

Titilayo Olubunmi Olaposi
African Institute for Science Policy and Innovation, Obafemi Awolowo University, Ile-Ife, Nigeria

*Address all correspondence to: olapositi@gmail.com

References

[1] Ugoani JNN, Ibeenwo GI (2015). Entrepreneurship development and employment generation in Nigeria: A Study of the National Directorate of Employment. Independent Journal of Management and Production. 2015; 6(3); 687-710.

[2] Doran J, McCarthy N, O'Connor M. The role of entrepreneurship in stimulating economic growth in developed and developing countries. Cogent Economics and Finance. 2018;6; 1442093.

[3] Eniola AA, Entebang H. Government Policy and Performance of Small and Medium Business Management. International Journal of Academic Research in Business and Social Sciences. 2015; 5(2); 237-248.

[4] Amadi VC, Ukoha O, Alagah KD. Government Entrepreneurship Development Programmes And Small & Medium Scale Enterprise Success in Rivers State. International Journal of Advanced Academic Research. 2018; 4(4); 202-219.

[5] Akinyemi FO, Adejumo OO. Government policies and Entrepreneurship Phases in Emerging Economies: Nigeria and South Africa. Journal of Global Entrepreneurship Research. 2018; 8(35); 1-18.

[6] Taiwo DO, Akinyode BF. Implications of Street Trading Activities on the Residents within Central Business Districts in Nigeria. IOSR Journal Of Humanities And Social Science (IOSR-JHSS). 2017; 22(2); 93-99.

[7] Brinkley C, Chrisinger B, Hillier A. Tradition of healthy food access in low-income neighborhoods: Price and variety of curbside produce trading compared to conventional retailers. Journal of Agricultural Food System Community Development. 2013; 4(1): 155-169.

[8] Anetor FO. An Investigation into the Value of Street Vending in Nigeria: A Case of Lagos State. Journal of Marketing and Consumer Research; 2015; 11; 35-40.

[9] Edeme RK, Nkalu NC. Operations of Street Food vendors and Their Impact on Sustainable Life in Rural Nigeria. American Economic and Social Review. 2018; 4(1): 1-7.

[10] Inolia MM. The impact of street trading on the economic development in the city of Polokwane, Limpopo Province. (Unpublished Master's thesis) University of Limpopo, Polokwane, Limpopo; 2016.

[11] Amegah AK, Jaakkola JJK. Street trading and waste picking in developing countries: a long-standing hazardous occupational activity of the urban poor. International Journal of Occupational and Environmental Health. 2016; 22(3); 187-192.

[12] Amoo EO, Ola-David O, Ogunrinola, IO, Fadayomi TO. Street Trading Activities ` and Maternal Health in Urban Areas of Nigeria. Global Journal of Human Social Sciences Arts & Humanities. 2012; 12(15); 47-55

[13] Olurinola, IO, Fadayomi T, Amoo EO, Ola-David O. Ocupational Health and Safety among Street Traders in Nigeria. International Journal of Economics and Finance. 2014; 6(4), 2014.

[14] Adedeji JA, Fadamiro JA., Adeoye AO. Spatial implications of street trading in Osogbo traditional city centre, Nigeria. Architecture Research, 2014; 4(1A); 34-44.

[15] Ashimolowo OR, Aromolaran AK, Inegbedion SO. Child street trading activities and Its effect on the educational attainment of its victims in Epe Local Government Area of Lagos

State. Journal of Agricultural Science. 2010; 2(4); 211-220.

[16] Ojo M, Olufemi D. A sociological investigation of the determinant factors and the effects of child street hawking in Nigeria: Agege, Lagos State, Under Survey. International Journal of Asian Social Science. 2013; 3(1);114-137.

[17] Clark CID, Yesufu S. Child street trading as an aspect of child abuse and neglect Oredo Municipality of Edo State, Nigeria As Case Study. European Scientific Journal. 2012; 8(5), 148-158.

[18] Ugochukwu EF, Okeke KN, Onubogu CU, Edokwe ES. Socio - demographic characteristics of child street vendors in Nnewi, Nigeria. Nigeria Journal of Paediatrics. 2012; 39(4); 174-178.

[19] Saiz-Alvarez JM, Vaquero MG. Entrepreneurship Concept, Theories, and New Approaches [Internet]. 2017. Available from: https://www.researchgate.net/publication/331832739. Accessed 2020-08-22.

[20] Okpara JO. (2011). Factors Constraining the growth and survival of SMEs in Nigeria: Implications for poverty alleviation. Management Research Review 2011; 34(2); 156-171.

[21] Hussain MD, Halim MSA. Micro Enterprise Development and Income Sustainability for Poverty Reduction: A Literature Investigation. International Journal of Business and Technopreneurship. 2017; 7(1): 23-38.

[22] Skinner C. AAPS planning education toolkit: the informal economy. Cape Town, South Africa: African Association of Planning Schools [Internet]. 2011. Available from www.inclusivecities.org. Accessed 2020-08-22.

[23] Wigan Council. Street Trading [Internet]. 2019. Available from www.wigan.gov.uk.Accesed 2020-08-22.

[24] Amoah-Mensah A. Street trading and competitive advantage: Towards building a theoretical framework. The Qualitative Report. 2016; 21(9); 1651-1673.

[25] Food and Agriculture Organization of the United Nations (FAO) [Internet] (2020). Street Foods. Available from: www.fao.org Accessed 2020-08-22..

[26] ILO (2018). *Women and men in the informal economy: A statistical picture.* Third Edition. International Labour Office, Geneva [Internet]. Available from https://www.ilo.org. Accessed 2020-08-23.

[27] OECD/ILO. Tackling Vulnerability in the Informal Economy, Development Centre Studies, OECD Publishing, Paris [Internet]. 2019. Available from https://doi.org/10.1787/939b7bcd-en. Accessed 2020-08-23.

[28] ILO. Women and men in the informal economy: A statistical picture. Third Edition. International Labour Office, Geneva [Internet]. Available from https://www.ilo.org. Accessed 2020-08-23.

[29] Baumann FA, Kaiser J. (2012). Interregional study vocational education and training (VET) in the informal sector [Internet]. 2012. Available from www.rifau.org/mediadb/9392/20308/EtudeComparativeInformel_eng.pdf. Accessed 2020-08-24.

[30] Baumann FA, Kaiser J. Interregional study vocational education and training (VET) in the informal sector [Internet]. 2012. Available from www.rifau.org/mediadb/9392/20308/EtudeComparativeInformel_eng.pdf. Accessed 2020-08-24.

[31] ILO. Women and men in the informal economy: A statistical picture. Third Edition. International Labour Office, Geneva [Internet]. 2018. Available from https://www.ilo.org. Accessed 2020-08-24.

[32] Bénit-Gbaffou. In Quest for Sustainable Models of Street Trading Management: Lessons for Johannesburg After Operation Clean Sweep. Johannesburg, South Africa: University of Witwatersrand, School of Architecture and Planning, Centre for Urbanism and Built Environment Studies. 2015.

[33] Castells M, Portes A. World underneath: the origins, dynamics and effects of the informal economy. In Portes A, Castells M, Benton LA, editors, The Informal Economy: studies in advanced and less developing countries. Baltimore: John Hopkins University Press; 1989. p. 19-42.

[34] Williams CC, Gurtoo A. Evaluating competing theories of street entrepreneurship: some lessons from a study of street vendors in Bangalore, India [Internet]. 2012.International Entrepreneurship and Management Journal. Available from http://ssrn.com/abstract=2706144. Accessed 2020-08-24.

[35] Williams CC, Gurtoo A. (2012). Evaluating competing theories of street entrepreneurship: some lessons from a study of street vendors in Bangalore, India [Internet]. 2012. International Entrepreneurship and Management Journal. Available from http://ssrn.com/abstract=2706144. Accessed 2020-08-24.

[36] Handoyo E, Setiawan AB. Street Vendors (PKL) as the Survival Strategy of Poor Community. Journal Ekonomi dan Kebijakan (Jejak). 2018; 11(1), 173-188.

[37] Cross J, Morales A, editors. Introduction: locating Street Markets in the Modern/Postmodern World. In: Street Entrepreneurs: People, Place and Politics in Local and Global Perspectives. Routledge, London. 2007.

[38] Cross JC. Street Vendors, Modernity and Postmodernity: Conflict and Compromise in the Global Economy. International Journal of Sociology and Social Policy. 2000. 20(1), 29-51.

[39] Oloukoi J, Oyinloye, RO, Yadjemi H. (2014). Geospatial analysis of urban sprawl in Ile-Ife, City, Nigeria. South African Journal of Geomatics, 2014; 3(2); 128-144.

[40] Official website of the State of Osun [Internet] 2020. Available from: htps://www.osun.gov.ng/home_about osun_majortowns_ile-ife. Accessed 2020-09-30.

[41] Collins CJ, Hanges P, Locke EA. The Relationship of Achievement Motivation to Entrepreneurial Behaviour: A Meta-Analysis. Human Performance. 2004. 17(1): 95-117.

[42] Timmons J. New Ventures Creation, Entrepreneurship in the 21st Century. Irwin McGraw-Hill, 1999. 27-30p.

[43] Ebitu ET, Basil G, Ufot JA. An Appraisal of Nigeria's Micro, Small and Medium Enterprises(MSMES): Growth, Challenges and Prospects. British Journal of Marketing Studies. 2016; 4(5); 21-36.

[44] National MSME Collaborative Survey (NMSMECS) (2010). Survey report on Micro, Small and Medium Enterprises (MSMEs) in Nigeria. Collaboration between national bureau of statistics and small and medium enterprise development agency of Nigeria (SMEDAN). 2010.

[45] SMEDAN. Guide to NEDEP on OLOP opportunities in Nigeria. Volume 1. February, 2014.

Section 2

Leading for Learning: How to Transform Organizations into Innovation

Chapter 6

Rethinking Innovative Learning Opportunities for Teachers in Educational Organizations toward Education 4.0

Süleyman Davut Göker and Mubeher Ürün Göker

Abstract

Teacher behaviors play a key role in forming and shaping organizational culture in schools. The current innovative and leadership-based learning objectives introduced by Education 4.0 have made the transformation obligatory from traditional classrooms of the industrial society to creation of digital classrooms. This transformation will embrace digital curriculum that might impact learning outcomes and reduce in-class management. How is it different from traditional classrooms? The spaces in a digital classroom are both digital and physical. This environment asks for future creative convergence talents, thus giving teachers new tasks to take greater ownership of change processes of their school culture. This shift also requires creation of reflective learning communities together with a redefinition of the meaning and scope of teacher supervision. This study introduces, a "Teacher Competency Development Model," in which innovative learning opportunities for teachers in educational organizations toward Education 4.0 are offered through innovative models in teacher supervision based on cognitive, reflective, and peer coaching and their utilization within the educational contexts. Within this framework, the contents and strategies of three supervision models, namely, reflective, cognitive, and peer coaching to be able to help teachers survive and cope with their adaptation to Education 4.0 will be discussed.

Keywords: redefinition of learning opportunities, teacher competency development model, Education 4.0, school culture, peer, cognitive and reflective coaching

1. Introduction

Teacher behaviors play a key role in forming and shaping organizational culture in schools. The current innovative and leadership-based learning objectives introduced by Education 4.0 have made the transformation obligatory from traditional classroom of the industrial society to creation of digital classrooms. The Fourth Industrial Revolution has taken people to an era of new social and unprecedented changes. In all sectors of all industries, today's hot issue is the Fourth Industrial Revolution. The First Industrial Revolution was based on the mechanization through the steam engine; the Second Industrial Revolution was based on mass production through electric energy; and the Third Industrial Revolution was based on intelligence information revolution through computer and internet. And the ongoing Fourth Industrial Revolution is based on IoT, Cloud, big data, AI, and mobiles. Also, in the near future, we will meet the 5G wireless network era. The speed of 5G is 280 times faster than LTE. And in some countries, this Fourth Industrial Revolution can be called digital transformation. **Figure 1** illustrates the advent of the Fourth Industrial Revolution (IR) age.

The Fourth Industrial Revolution makes three major changes namely intellectualization of human and machine, virtualization of the real and virtual, and hyper connection of human and things. This revolution brings about changes in future society due to technological progress. Technological progress includes infinite increase in data as well as explosive growth of network. This technological progress will bring increase in value of data and according to these changes the future society will evolve toward role change between humans and machines. In particular, we need to note the increasing data value, which will become more important in the near future.

Within this framework, we need to discuss the global change trends to respond to the Fourth Industrial Revolution. First of all, adaptability is more critical to success than ever. In other words, the importance of the user experience is growing and growing. Additionally, as the amount of data increases, big data management and analytics will become more important. For example, in 2027, bitcoin and the blockchain will become very popular in the business fields. With regard to the key success factors, we need to look at three aspects: technology, industry, and society.

From a technological point of view, technology will evolve into "High Intelligence Information Tech" and "High Quality Data Infrastructure" and provide high-quality intelligent information technologies to industry. And with technological assistance, the whole industry will achieve intelligent information.

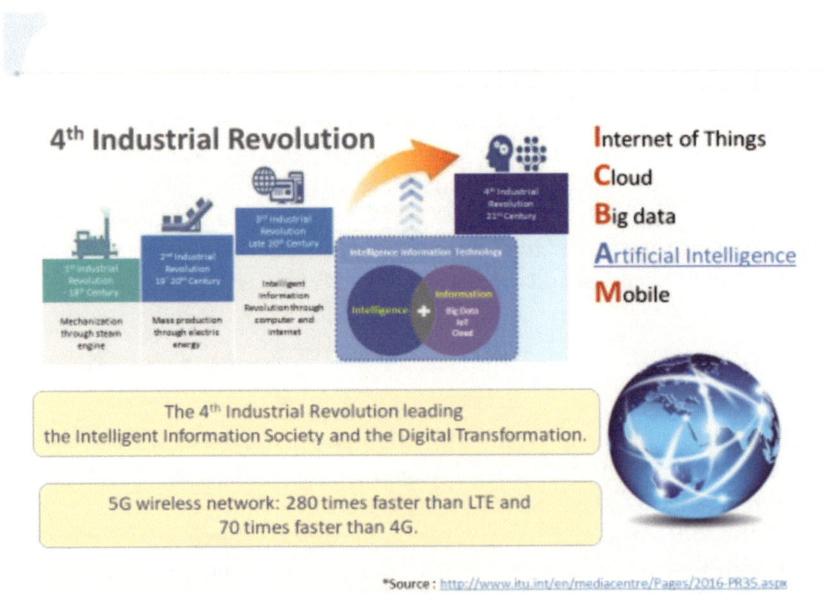

Figure 1.
The advent of the fourth industrial revolution (IR) age.

2. What Education 4.0 proposes

As far as the educational innovation in the Fourth Industrial Revolution era is concerned, these changes have accelerated many things and respective and unique skilled sets of human capital have been required by the different conditions of social economy. The important factor in the future intelligent information society is to cultivate human-tech literacy resources. The importance of development of the required skills lies in people in learning management, to develop the skills as well as knowledge abilities taking the needs of the society into consideration [1]. Leapfrog [2] called the education in this era responding to the agrarian society as Education 1.0, industrial society as Education 2.0, globalization as Education 3.0, and innovation as Education 4.0.

To be able to cultivate human-tech literacy resources in the future intelligent information society, new and creative fusion talents are required. These creative fusion talents should have the following four intelligences: context intelligence, emotional intelligence, social emotion intelligence, and physical intelligence as indicated in **Figure 2**.

As can be seen in **Figure 2**, the intelligences traditionally known as multiple intelligences within the theory of multiple intelligences developed in Gardner [3] (logical-mathematical, linguistic, bodily-kinesthetic, musical, spatial, intrapersonal, interpersonal, and naturalist intelligence) look to have been reshaped and focus has been given on social, physical, context, and emotional intelligence with a new understanding. This shift will bring many changes in learning and teaching theories currently being followed as well.

From today on, we will be discussing creative talent cultivation through fusion education together with the introduction of the importance of these four intelligences with more emphasis on various ICT-based learning models. These learning models will also replace traditionally known learning models used in different educational contexts. These various kinds of learning models are evolving based

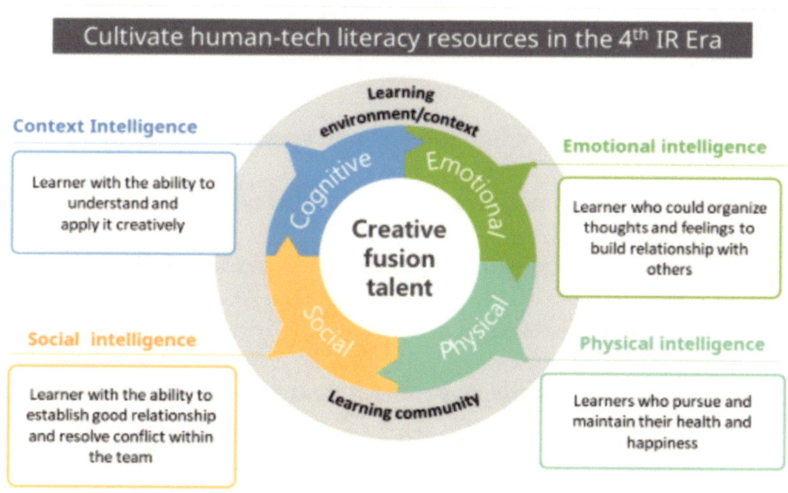

Figure 2.
Creative fusion talents for future intelligent information society.

on mobile. Particularly, in some countries, mobile has become commonplace beyond the PC. **Figure 3** describes the diversification of digital learning in the Fourth IR era.

The learning models given in **Figure 3** also include various elements of learning ecosystem to provide optimized learning system to each learner in response to the Fourth Industrial Revolution. This learning ecosystem has to be considered to promote innovative and optimized learning. This innovative and optimized learning introduces change trends of educational digital contents. Nowadays, digital content is evolving in the following six directions. 1. Interactive, 2. Characteristic, 3. Clipped (mobile-based), 4. Global, 5. Realistic (AR/VR embedded), and 6. Emotional.

Almost each of these directions gives a special focus on coding education. In the Fourth Industrial Revolution era, the importance of coding education is emphasized around the world in following ways:

1. Coding is the building block of the future.

2. Learning code is your gateway into understanding how to make the future yours.

3. The coding really determines how it will look on the screen. Learning to code will guarantee that your vision gets carried through to completion.

4. Behind code is a bunch more 1s and 0s that do the real work inside the brain of the computer. Code is a fascinating world of its own.

5. Coding will change the way you think.

6. Code will give you a fresh way to look at problems. Code is a lot like structured poetry and will change the way you see the world through computational thinking.

To sum up, the future education direction is to create a leading country of intelligence information society with creative fusion talents. This change trend also redefines the objectives of future of education in the following reflected ways:

1. Education to maximize student interest and aptitude

2. Education for thinking, problem-solving, and creativity

3. Customized education considering individual learning ability

4. Education to raise key talents in intelligence information technology

5. Education to focus on people and contribute to social integration.

From the stand point of educational innovation for the intelligent information society, the content and objectives of educational system in the world seem to move beyond rote education to realize problem-solving and critical-thinking centered education. This will require an expansion of SW/STEAM education and fulfilling computational thinking-oriented education and a reorganization of curriculum and system overall for developing autonomous competency and supporting future preparation. Establishing an adaptive learning system using intelligent information

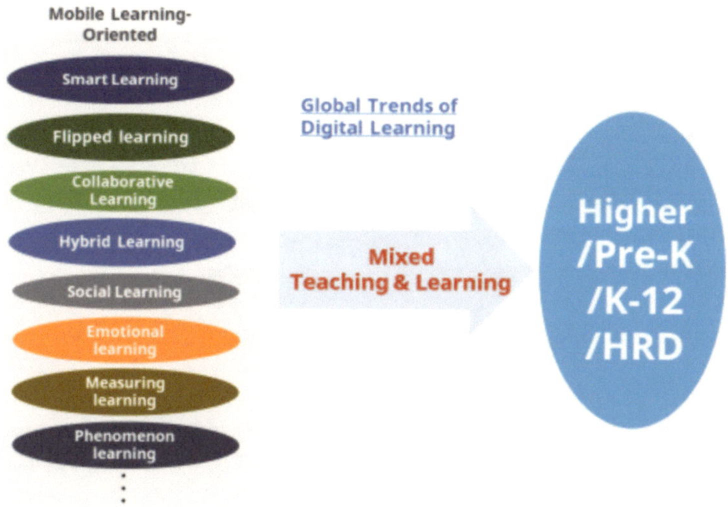

Figure 3.
Diversification of digital learning in fourth IR era.

technology will also set up an adaptive learning system by analyzing history and level to maximize learning efficacy.

These chain changes will develop intelligence learning platform to support activities for advanced learning according to individual interest and level and create a core personnel specializing in intelligent IT that is capable of leading new industries. These systems are expected to raise intelligence information talents who are good at computer science, data analytics, and SW development (foster talented children in intelligent information area).

Furthermore, these new trends will also have implications for universities. For example, industry-university-research collaboration intensive learning courses with top faculties will be opened and the quality gains of the students registered in these courses will naturally support best graduation schools in intelligence information technology area.

3. A teacher competency development program for the future

Development of direction of cloud-based intelligent personalized learning service will consider new assessments based on individual service, service beneficiary, visualized technology, AI platform technology and resource. For example, in the case of individual service, online activity, analytics, assessment/diagnosis, and so on will be implemented. These will bring new insights into the evaluation of student products and learning outcomes. Because data will be collected based on learner's use and learning activities, and analytics results are recommended for optimized personalized learning. However, older teachers will hesitate to use new learning methods or new ICT-based devices.

Above all, in order to cultivate future creative convergence talents, a teacher competency development program for the future is needed. Within this framework, we need to rethink innovative learning opportunities for teachers in educational organizations toward Education 4.0. To be able to create these

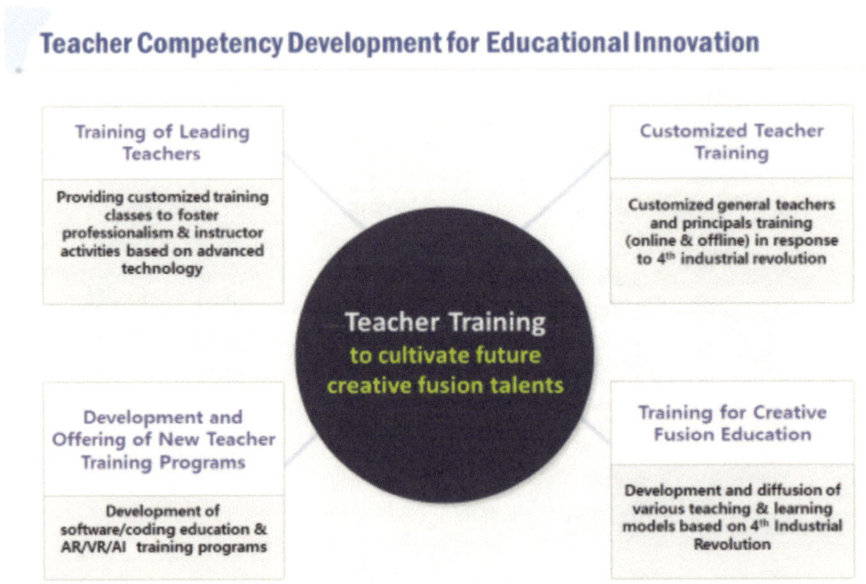

Figure 4.
Teacher competency development for educational innovation.

innovative learning environments for teachers, we should train teachers and expand infrastructure for the intelligent information society. Additionally, we should commit customized training of S/W education for teachers' continuous reinforcement of SW capacity. Doing so, we will also supply wireless internet network in all schools and develop high-tech future school model using AI, AR, and VR. The content and areas of teacher competency development are summarized in **Figure 4**.

As can be seen in **Figure 4**, this teacher competency development can be realized with "Training of Leading Teachers," "Customized Teacher Training," "Development and Offering of New Teacher Training Programs," and "Training for Creative Convergence Education."

4. Innovative teacher supervision models within the teacher competency development for educational innovation

The huge transformation in learning and teaching models, digital classroom, and educational contexts will bring a radical change in teacher behaviors. For the teachers to change, creation of reflective learning communities is required together with a redefinition of the meaning and scope of teacher supervision. Such a change would only be possible through development of new coaching skills, which would require development of reflective and cognitive skills of the teachers themselves and peer coaching environments to be able to survive and cope with their adaptation to Education 4.0 within the educational contexts. Serving teacher development and collaboration for better learning and teaching, this model will also change teacher behaviors and it will help reshaping. Within this framework, three supervision models namely, reflective, cognitive, and peer coaching to be able help teachers survive and cope with their adaptation to Education 4.0 will be discussed.

4.1 Reflective coaching (reflection: a great asset for a teacher competency development for the future)

The fourth industrial based on changes such as intellectualization of human and machine, virtualization of reality and virtual and hyper connection of human and things and its reflections on Education 4.0 are catering to the needs of the learners and teachers in "innovative era." These require changes in behaviors with certain features of connectivism, parallelism [4], and visualization. The learner's ability should be developed through this learning management for the sake of applying the new technology. According to Sinlarat [1], the learning management mentioned looks to be a new learning system, which will allow learners to grow with knowledge and skills to survive during their whole life and they will be equipped with the best of their abilities. From this perspective, Education 4.0 would be more than just an education. On the other hand, learning management is expected to cope with the changes in economic and social and environments to serve the human capital need. To be able to achieve this, a change would be needed in learning management, which requires reflection. Through reflection and reflective learning environments, teachers would have a great opportunity to self-evaluate their reflective teaching practices. Because, they can raise their professional development as long as they become more aware of their weaknesses as well as strengths in their actual teaching practices.

From this point of view, reflection could be regarded as a powerful tool to reflect and change and it could be conducted with some methods [5]. According to some scholarly works, it could be achieved through reflective practices, which would allow teachers to grow professionally [6]. Schön [7] named reflective practice as a critical process in refining a person's artistry and crafting a certain discipline. In other words, this process requires a person to see his or her experiences in practice while being observed and coached by other people. Smyth [8] maintains that there are four serial stages regarding questions, which lead a teacher to critical reflection:

1. Describing—What do I do?

2. Informing—What is the meaning of this?

3. Confronting—How did I come to be like this?

4. Constructing—In what other ways could I do it?

These types of reflective practices are utilized in both in-service and pre-service education and peer involvement and coaching are regarded as two essential parts of reflective practices observed mostly in pre-service education for teachers [9]. In this study, our focus will be on journals for individual reflective practices, collaborative learning, video or audio recordings of lessons, teacher educator's feedback, student feedback, action research, study groups for reflective practice of small groups, teacher portfolios, instructional rounds, classroom walk-throughs for school-based reflective practice, and cognitive coaching and peer coaching even though different approaches to each type of reflective practice are available.

4.1.1 Strategies to practice reflection

To have a brief understanding of the content and functions of reflective coaching, one needs to find out the reflective instruments and strategies employed during the teacher evaluation. The preliminary stage before the reflective process is to collect data about what is actually happening in classes. There are some options to do that:

- **Reflective journals/diaries:** This could be regarded as the easiest way to initiate the reflective process because it is completely personal. Through the use of journals to create reflective learning environments, Göker [10] argues that teachers could provide other teachers with some opportunities to reflect on their actual practices. Within this framework, writing diaries is often used in various learning environments. In writing diaries, teachers would basically express his or her feelings, ideas, and reflections considering their own teaching practice. Doing so, teachers could keep notes in learning logs or personal narratives, dialog journals including various reflections providing them with a critical understanding of how they act in classes and assisting them in realizing other alternative strategies to develop their own practice.

- **Collaborative learning**: According to Brookfield [11], an ongoing communication with the peers created in mutually cooperative environment is essential. This type of collaborative work with peers is expected to contribute to development of reflective thought among teachers. Through efficient discussions, teachers could report their experiences and reframe, and check to broaden their vision about the practices. These would bring changes in teacher behaviors and the school culture could change naturally.

- **Video or audio recordings of lessons**: Recording of lessons could present quality data for the reflective practice. After watching these recordings of their own or other peer members, teachers could develop better awareness of their own teaching. Because, many things happen in classes and teachers may not be aware of what is actually happening and teachers may not normally see. Within this perspective, this type of recording could present a clearer picture about the whole process of teaching. Discussions to be made would trigger a teacher's reflective thought, reflecting on their strengths and weaknesses, thus helping them get some inspiration toward their development in their teaching.

- **Teacher educator's feedback:** This type of feedback would assist the teachers in reflecting upon their lessons, tasks, and activities in the school culture.

- **Student feedback**: Students in classes could also give more information about what is actually happening in classes. Teachers could ask their students to present information about what is going on in classes, because, students' perceptions and opinions could present a different and valuable perspective.

- **Action research**: Seeing it as a reflective process, a teacher could find out progressive responses and solutions to problems to understand his or her practice and develop the ways they address issues. This type of reflective process would help teachers to develop more awareness about what is actually happening in classes by means of defining the main problems and speculating on prospective causes and solutions. They would then attempt to initiate a proper action plan.

- **Study groups for reflective practice of small groups:** This type of formation of groups has been utilized since colonial times, the first of which was documented in America by Franklin [12]. The basic aim then was to search for better business practices. These groups were organized and utilized for teacher development to serve the quality of teaching by means of professional reading, dialog in the 1980s [6, 13–15] (Little, 1981). To achieve their objectives, 5–10 teachers form a group to begin discussions on a defined topic or curriculum, methodology, and testing to be able to compare and review their own experiences and to seek answers to implement new things in their future teaching practices. The members highly value class observations and they come together after observation to discuss the issues targeted before. This approach is still followed during post-conference sessions of today's cognitive and peer coaching implementations.

- **Teacher portfolios:** They were first initiated and utilized professionally after the formation of a professional model for teachers by the NBPTS (The National Board for Professional Teaching Standards) seeking national certification [16]. To achieve teaching standards, experienced teachers [17] wishing to get the highest honor in teaching profession came together.

- **Instructional rounds:** These rounds have recently been initiated by City et al. [18]. They attempted to adapt and extend on health practices to be able to develop their knowledge and practices through observations, analysis, and discussions conducted with other physicians. School principals and supervisors employed a similar method to create a learning environment serving the progressive solutions to problems to improve instruction together with the teachers and develop their teaching practices. They carried out four different steps consisting of identifying a problem, observing, debriefing, and taking corrective steps [18]. Their aim was to form a reflective culture through the use of a common language among each other. Within this framework, a cultural reflective transformation was targeted to create a reflective learning environment, in which they would reshape teacher behaviors. They did it as a type of reflection-for action because they aimed to improve teaching practices within a system.

- **Classroom walk-throughs for school-based reflective practice:** Classroom walk-through, as a supervisory technique and a type of reflection on action, was first initiated in educational settings in the 1990s [19]. Supervisors visit classes to observe classes and evaluate practices of teaching and learning outcomes. Professional dialogs between supervisors and teachers consist of dialog, focus on what is actually happening in classes are highly valued [18]. Follow-up dialogs conducted in reflective in nature are expected to move teachers to achieve a certain level of reflection and collaboration to teaching practices.

4.2 Cognitive coaching

This type of coaching model was first initiated by Costa and Garmston [20] as a critical and "nonjudgmental mediation of thinking" based on constructivist learning theory. The ultimate goal is to foster a person's capacity to improve abilities of self-monitoring, self-directedness as well as those of self-modification. Planning conversation, observation, and reflecting conversation basically constitute a three-stage coaching cycle. The model described as a teacher supervision means in this study is mainly based on (a) the theories by Bandura [21] and Vygotsky [22], (b) application of the researcher's model of peer coaching [9] and model of reflective coaching [10, 23] implemented within different educational contexts, and (c) similar mentoring or coaching studies.

During the coaching process, a competent coach (mentor) is regarded as an essential figure with a capacity to: (1) create interactions with the participants giving priority to produce self-directed learning; (2) seek trust in maintaining coaching relationships; (3) evaluate and intercede the five states of mind; and finally (4) produce new approaches to foster the five states of mind to be able to create a learning environment, in which the trainees could mediate the capacity of their own and that of others to develop. Cognitive coaching, within this process, could also be described as a formative model to promote teacher self-evaluation to help them develop their self-efficacy, identity, and teaching skills. From this perspective, it is important to ease reflective process and possible responses coming from the mentee, the mentor in this study drafts questions. To be able to produce any cognitive development, a good mentor should use paralanguage, structuring as well as meditative questioning response behaviors [20]. The four strategies given above are always utilized during both the planning and reflective conversation sessions to help the mentees give the most suitable decisions about their teaching practices. A teacher could also be provided autonomy to a certain extent and this would ease their professional development conducted through cognitive coaching.

4.3 Peer coaching

Peer coaching is regarded as a part of reflective process and a fruitful tool to create collaborative efforts and it warrants consideration as a potentially serviceable solution for improving teacher effectiveness when implemented both in pre-service and in-service teaching settings. Peer coaching as almost the most basic supervision mode employed in classes is regarded as a clinical and reflective process, in which teacher teams or student teachers regularly observe themselves for the sake of refining teaching practice, encouraging reflective practice, providing assistance, suggestions, and support [9, 24, 25]. This process is considered as a tool for the more experienced teachers to use the skills they gained during their in-service teacher program. Research also advocates the use of peer coaching implementations to empower transfer of training to real teaching practice in classes, supercharging collegiality by means of peers' exchange of feedback together with reflective development of teachers [9, 25].

The most common way of peer coaching is conducted in the following way: A teacher invites his or her peer to monitor his/her class to collect data about what is really happening in class. This could be done through note taking, checklist, a narrative agreed, a simple observation task, and drawing conclusions. The teacher could ask his/her peer to put emphasis on, for example, what different patterns of interaction occur or which students contribute the most in the lesson. It is better for the observer not to be involved in evaluating the teacher's lesson for the sake of having a positive evaluation. Coaching benefits and expectations are negotiated between the peers during a pre-conference and post-conference.

Taking the recent developments and changes in Education 4.0, Göker [9] argues that these peer coaching environments could play a key role in creating the required reflective learning communities, in which teachers and teacher candidates would be trained as practitioners to lead to change. Göker [9] further maintains that one strategy for development of teachers mostly suitable for the creation of a reflective learning community is that of peer coaching, described as the process of two peers studying on planning instruction, developing support materials, and monitoring each other's work with students. Within this framework, peer coaching is regarded as nonjudgmental, based on classroom observation followed by feedback, and intended to develop teaching skills. Openness and trust are the two essential characteristics of peer coaching process and peers need to be sensitive to be non-evaluative or nonjudgmental during the pre/post-conference sessions, in which they discuss, share their own experiences, teaching, and learning behaviors as well as teaching practices.

5. Conclusion

Any change in teacher behavior, which plays a key role in forming and shaping organizational culture in schools, is not an easy task. From the stand point of educational innovation for the intelligent information society, promoting reflective practices and developing professional learning communities through reflective, cognitive, and peer coaching implementations is essential to lead to a teacher change. The current innovative and leadership-based learning objectives introduced by Education 4.0 have made it obligatory for teachers to change. As Education 4.0 environments require future creative convergence talents, teachers should carry out new tasks to take greater ownership of growing creative convergence talents and to change processes of their school culture. This change process could be achieved through creating reflective learning communities together with a redefinition of the meaning and scope of teacher supervision. For the sake of achieving these changes in teacher behaviors, this study discussed a "Teacher Competency Development Model," in which, innovative learning opportunities for teachers in educational organizations were offered through innovative models in teacher supervision based on cognitive, reflective, and peer coaching and their utilization within the educational contexts. It is obvious that if teachers create a professional and reflective learning community aiming at behavioral change in reflective practices and promoting professional development, learning becomes self-directed and they definitely become empowered thorough learning management, which looks to be an essential task required by Education 4.0. Today, we have a digital society and life style has changed. Learning management needs to respond to the prospective changes of behaviors of both teachers and learners.

Author details

Süleyman Davut Göker[1*] and Mubeher Ürün Göker[2]

1 Faculty of Education, Çanakkale Onsekiz Mart University, Turkey

2 School of Foreign Languages, Canakkale Onsekiz Mart University, Turkey

*Address all correspondence to: gokersd@gmail.com

References

[1] Sinlarat P. Education 4.0 is more than education. In: Annual Academic Seminar of the Teacher's Council 2016 on the Topic of Research of the Learning Innovation and Sustainable Educational Management. Bangkok: The Secretariat Office of Teacher's Council; 2016

[2] Harkins AM. Leapfrog principles and practices: Core components of education 3.0 and 4.0. Futures Research Quarterly. 2008;**24**(1):19-31

[3] Gardner H. Frames of Mind: The Theory of Multiple Intelligences. New York: Basic Books; 1983

[4] Goldie JGS. Connectivism: A knowledge learning theory for the digital age? Medical Teacher. 2016;**38**(10):1064-1069. DOI: 10.3109/0142159X.2016.1173661

[5] Fullan M. Leadership and Sustainability: System Thinkers in Action. Thousand Oaks, CA: Corwin Press, Inc; 2005

[6] York-Barr J, Sommers WA, Ghere GS, Montie J. Reflective Practice to Improve Schools: An Action Guide for Educators. Thousand Oaks, CA: Corwin Press, Inc.; 2001

[7] Schon DA. The Reflective Practitioner: How Professionals Think in Action. New York, NY: Basic Books, Inc.; 1983

[8] Smyth J. Developing and sustaining critical reflection in teacher education. Journal of Teacher Education. 1989;**40**(2):2-9

[9] Göker SD. Impact of peer coaching on self-efficacy and instructional skills in TEFL teacher education. System, And International Journal of Educational Technology and Applied Linguistics. 2006;**34**(2):239-254

[10] Göker SD. Use of reflective journals in development of teachers' leadership and teaching skills. Universal Journal of Educational Research. 2016;**4**(12A):63-70. DOI: 10.13189/ujer.2016.041309. Available from: http://www.hrpub.org

[11] Brookfield S. Becoming a Critically Reflective Teacher. San-Francisco: Jossey-Bass. 1995

[12] Makibbin SS, Sprague MM. Study groups: Conduit for reform. A paper presented at the meeting of the National Staff Development Council. In: St. Santa CGS, Smith K, editors. Teachers are Researchers: Reflection and Action. Newark, DE: International Reading Association; 1991

[13] Cooper C, Boyd J. Creating sustained professional development. In: Brody C, Davidson N, editors. Professional Development for Cooperative Learning: Issues and Approaches. Albany, NY: State University of New York Press; 1998

[14] Stigler JW, Hiebert J. The Teaching Gap: Best Ideas from the World's Teachers for Improving Education in the Classroom. New York, NY: Free Press; 1999

[15] Little JW. School Success in Staff Development: The Role of Staff Development in Urban Desegregated Schools. Boulder, CO: Center for Action Research. 1981

[16] Bullock AA, Hawk PP. Developing a Teaching Portfolio: A Guide for Preservice and Practicing Teachers. Upper Saddle River, NJ: Pearson Prentice Hall; 2005

[17] National Board for Professional Teaching Standards. 2009. Available from: http://www.nbpts.org [Accessed: 15 July 2016]

[18] City EA, Elmore RF, Fiarman SE, Teitel L. Instructional Rounds in Education: A Network Approach to Improving Teaching and Learning. Cambridge, MA: Harvard Education Press; 2009

[19] Downey C, English F, Frase L, Poston W, Steffy B. The Three-Minute Classroom Walk-through. Thousand Oaks, CA: Corwin Press; 2004

[20] Costa A, Garmston R. Cognitive Coaching: A Foundation for Renaissance Schools. Norwood, MA: Christopher-Gordon Publishers; 2002

[21] Bandura A. Self-efficacy: Toward a unifying theory of behavioral change. Psychological Review. 1997;**84**:191-215

[22] Vygotsky LS. Mind in Society: The Development of Higher Psychological Processes. Cambridge, MA: Harvard University Press. 1978. Available from: http://ouleft.org/wp-content/uploads/Vygotsky-Mind-in-Society.pdf

[23] Göker SD. Reflective leadership in EFL. Theory and Practice in Language Studies. 2012;**2**(8):1355-1362

[24] Joyce B, Showers B. Improving inservice training: The messages of research. Educational Leadership. 1980;**37**(1980):379-385

[25] Thorn A, McLeod M, Goldsmith M. Peer coaching overview. 2007. Retrieved from: http://www.marshallgoldsmithlibrary.com [Accessed: 13 November 2019]

Chapter 7

Communication and Organizational Culture

Halvor Nordby

Abstract

When people in an organization understand themselves and their context of interaction from very different perspectives, there is an increased risk of poor organizational dialogue. The reason is not only that individuals' social interpretations of others are influenced by their idiosyncratic perspectives. In interactions involving a significant diversity of individual perspectives, there is also a risk that communicators form radically different interpretations of goals and processes in the organization. It is therefore of crucial importance that people have a sufficiently similar understanding of action-guiding information, communicative acts and the workplace itself. The chapter focuses on the importance of creating shared organizational culture on the basis of four communication conditions from social interaction theory. (1) In communicative processes, senders need to secure the attention of audiences. (2) Senders and audiences need to have a sufficiently similar understanding of the language that is used. (3) Senders and audiences need to interpret communicative acts in a sufficiently similar way. (4) The attitudes and values that audiences ascribe to senders must correspond to the values and attitudes that senders actually have. After having clarified these conditions, the chapter applies them to analyse fundamental organizational challenges. The final part of the chapter argues that the conditions can, typically on management levels, constitute conceptual tools for creating unifying communicative cultures. Furthermore, using the conditions (1)–(4) actively as a means for securing communication across a diversity of individual perspectives can contribute to reaching organizational goals, no matter how they are defined.

Keywords: organizational communication, shared understanding, philosophy of language, cultural interaction, methodological tools

1. Introduction

One of the key concepts in communication theory is *horizons of understanding*. The concept refers to individuals' overall cognitive, emotional and experiential perspectives on themselves. It denotes the totality of mental states—representational and non-representational—that an individual has at a given time [1–3].

Defined like this, it is not difficult to understand why the concept of a subjective horizon has received a lot of attention in theories of organizational communication: Communicative challenges typically arise when communicators understand each other from very different perspectives [4, 5]. Such differences do not only shape individuals' interpretation of others. They can, even more fundamentally, create barriers of meaning connected to the language that is used. In such cases, the meaning a sender uses a communicative act to express in a communicative process is not the same as the meaning the audience associates with the act [6–8].

Differences in horizons can be intrinsically personal, and they can be connected to individual values and idiosyncratic preferences. However, and this is particularly interesting from a cultural perspective on organizations, differences can also be traced to formal and informal roles and positions [9, 10]. Consider for instance typical relations between managers and employees working in frontline services in organizations. Managers have, in many ways, a top-down perspective on frontline organizational challenges and employees' roles. Frontline employees, on the other hand, typically have a bottom-up point of view, closely connected to their roles and experiences in the organization [11–13]. This positional difference can make it difficult to reach aims of shared understanding in manager-employee dialogue about job tasks, principles of efficiency and quality aims [14, 15].

These kinds of communicative challenges related to organizational roles and positions can be analysed from various analytical perspectives. In this chapter, I focus on how different horizons of understanding can affect dialogue and social interaction understood as fundamental communicative processes. I will, more specifically, distinguish between four communication conditions: (1) the need to have attention, (2) the need to have a shared language, (3) the need to avoid associative misinterpretation and (4) the need to communicate attitudes, emotions and experiences.

After having clarified these conditions, I will argue that they can contribute to explain how organizational culture can be improved in two ways: From a descriptive perspective, the conditions can be used to understand the significance of having a shared communicative practice as an essential part of a well-functioning organizational culture. From a normative perspective, they can be used, on personal and system-based levels, as conceptual tools to strengthen communicative cultures. Fundamentally, I will conclude that collective knowledge and application of basic communication principles can improve the efficiency of organizations.

2. Background

It is widely recognized that communication is vital for organizational functioning [16–18]. If the communication within an organization is poor, then it is difficult to find adequate solutions to organizational challenges. If the communication is good, then the probability of efficient organizational performance is improved, no matter how the goals and aims of the organization are defined [19]. When he was asked about the secret of his success, August Busch, CEO of one of America's most successful companies, famously said in an interview with *Forbes Magazine* (June 23, 1997): 'You're going to laugh at this ... it sounds so simple – but the key is communicate, communicate, communicate'.

The issue of how organizational efficiency depends on efficient communication has been explored in a number of ways [15, 20]. Many theorists have, in particular, analysed how communicative challenges typically arise in organizations and why it is of fundamental importance to meet these challenges [12, 15, 21]. On a general level, it is possible to categorize the challenges into two types:

- Exchange of information—how knowledge and action-guiding norms are conveyed, interpreted and implemented throughout an organization

- Relational communication—how people understand each other as autonomous subjects with attitudes, concerns, values and experiences

The informational and relational dimensions of human communication can be addressed from a variety of perspectives. In organizational contexts, two important sources of analysis are theories of communication and empirical studies of the diversity of understanding within organizations [22, 23].

Within the theoretical perspectives, a core idea has been the conditional that if communicators in organizations have very different individual perspectives, then it is difficult to secure efficient communication. Inconsistent or even incommensurable perspectives, many theorists have argued, will necessarily influence interaction, cooperation and organizational efficiency and undermine goals of performance [9, 20, 24].

Empirical studies have established that the antecedent of the theoretical conditional is, *de facto*, correct. Furthermore, the empirical research has not only shown how there is diversity of individual and group perspectives in different types of organizations but also contributed to explaining why this so and what the consequences are. A number of studies have, in particular, explored how barriers of communication are caused by individual and system-based factors and how these barriers have negative consequences for organizational performance [15, 24, 25].

The importance of implementing empirical knowledge about negative consequences of communicative barriers in organizational analysis has been thought of as essential [26, 27]. Generally, in social interpretation, it is impossible for communicators to step out of their idiosyncratic first-person perspectives—no person can see himself entirely from the outside. It is therefore not possible to avoid being influenced by one's own perspective in social interpretation [28, 29]. Arenas of interaction in organizations are no exception. As long as social interaction in organizations involves human beings with thoughts, beliefs, values and attitudes, one has to accept that it is of fundamental importance in organization theory to address communicative challenges related to gaps of subjective meaning and different idiosyncratic perspectives [30].

Recognition of the need to focus extensively on the diversity of understanding has led many theorists to focus on the relational 'soft side' of management and leadership [13]. The empirical studies of communicative challenges have also been a main source for the interest in relational aspects of organizations and human resource management [31, 32]. Within this tradition, many theorists have, on the basis of normative theories, elucidated how it is possible to reach aims of agreement and cooperation across gaps of understanding in organizations. These analyses have, in turn, been used to develop practical models for securing efficient organizational communication.

2.1 Shared horizons

In the philosophical literature on social interaction, many have argued that having partially shared horizons is a precondition for communication [1]. This has been connected not only to Hans Georg Gadamer's [2] theory of consensus as a condition for understanding. In the context of epistemology, aims related to shared horizons have also been connected to Jurgen Habermas and his theory of deliberate interaction. While Gadamer's theory concerns the basis for meaningful dialog, Habermas is more concerned with how communicators need to be able to communicate freely and rationally in order to get shared knowledge about a topic of discourse [29].

Hermeneutical analyses of the kind developed by Gadamer and Habermas have typically been applied on an individual explanatory level: The analyses have been used as frameworks to clarify what individuals can do to improve communication and how they can get the same kind of understanding about a topic of discourse [33, 34]. Nevertheless, it is widely recognized that the hermeneutical analyses also apply on group levels of explanations. For instance, a professional group will often need to understand other group perspectives in order to reach agreement about routines on interdisciplinary work. In organizational theory, conceptual resources from Gadamer and Habermas have been used to discuss such challenges along a number of dimensions, most notably to understand tensions and conflicts that arise when groups' horizons become too heterogenous [23].

Communicative conditions for organizational efficiency have not only been linked to the general concept of knowledge understood as justified true belief [35]. They have also been connected to various kinds of more specific knowledge. Furthermore, knowledge can be explicit—literally expressed in words. But knowledge can also be implicit and visible more indirectly through what people do. As described by Bermudez [36], this kind of knowledge is grounded in 'principles that guide our social behaviour and social understanding in those situations where we are not explicitly deploying the concepts and tools of propositional attitude psychology'. It is, in short, knowledge that is non-conceptualized [37].

Another dualism related to knowledge is the distinction between formalized and practical knowledge [38]. Knowledge that is part of a formal framework is not necessarily the knowledge that, in fact, governs practices. Formal knowledge might be poorly related to practice, and formal knowledge does not necessarily capture action preferences.

The distinction between formalized and practical knowledge [38] has often been used to analyse challenges related to transmission of information across levels of knowledge. Knowledge that people have on one level of an organization is not always known on other levels—even when the knowledge would have been important on those levels [30]. This type of problem has typically been addressed in discussions of interaction between managers and frontline employees in organizations. In particular, economic-administrative knowledge on management levels is not always understood in frontline groups, and experiential and professional judgement-based knowledge in frontline groups is not always adequately understood on management levels [13, 39].

No matter what the causes of this kind of decoupling are, gaps of knowledge can have a number of dramatic negative consequences [16, 25]. It is, after all, first-line professionals that directly deliver the product or service of the organization. Securing efficient 'vertical' information exchange and, more generally, good cooperation and shared knowledge is therefore of crucial importance. This is, to a large extent, a management responsibility [9].

2.2 Organizational culture

The concept of organizational knowledge has many dimensions, related to contexts of interaction and the abovementioned challenges [11]. There is, however, a general and close conceptual link between the concept of organizational knowledge and organizational culture. The latter concept has been defined in various ways in the literature, but the majority of definitions fall under Schein's [40] famous short characterization of organizational culture as 'This is how we do it here'.

Understood like this, the concept denotes what people actually do in an organization, not necessarily what they say they do or what written information to the external world outside the organization describe what people in the organization do [41, 42]. Schein's more precise definition is well known:

> *The culture of a group can now be defined as a pattern of shared assumptions learned by a group as it solves its problems of external adaption and internal integration, which has worked well enough to be considered valid and, therefore, to*

> *be taught to new members as the correct way to perceive, think and feel in relation to those problems.* (*[40], p. 18*)

The key concept here is shared practices. Organizational culture is manifested in collective action, it is action guiding, and it is often implicit: It cannot be explicated as surface knowledge or norms in collective practices. Just like implicit knowledge, as I explained this concept above, organizational culture is non-conceptualized and essentially tied to actions that are not directly governed by formal frameworks.

Schein calls this dimension of organizational culture for 'tacit, taken-for-granted, underlying assumptions', and he argues that 'unless you dig down to the level of the basic assumptions, you cannot really decipher [the culture] ... On the other hand, if you find some of those basic assumptions and explore their relationship, you are really getting at the essence of the culture and can then explain a great deal of what goes on' ([40], p. 53).

Consequently, one might say that if an organization expresses a certain external profile to the outside world—for instance to a group of clients or stakeholders—but nevertheless is governed by very different basic assumptions on the 'inside', then the main identifier of the organizational culture are those 'inside' assumptions, not the descriptions that are communicated externally. And the culture is a substantial driving force; it is a main 'engine' in the organization. Cultural practices have a large impact on how organizations actually work and how they function economically and reach performance goals [43].

Given the correlation between a 'good' culture and efficiency, the need to form a communicative platform is obvious: People need be able to communicate in order to share cultural frameworks. The point generalises to social interaction in organizations: Achieving aims of shared understanding is the key to getting people to cooperate.

In particular, this significance of organizational culture is salient in conceptions that emphasize that dialogue is the glue that ties a culture together. As Eisenberg and Riley ([43], pp. 294–295) notes, 'a communicative view of organizational culture sees communication as constitutive of culture'. This conception of culture as a communicative practice opens up for a variety of descriptive analyses, first and foremost on structural levels, in the sense that a communication perspective 'acknowledges the symbolic character of ordinary language and the ways in which cultural meanings are coconstructed in everyday conversation' [43]. However, explanations of how culture is a communicative practice can also be tied to individual levels, particularly connected to how 'the practical interests of organizational members seeking to enhance their effectiveness' [43].

3. Communication theory

How should the idea of communicative glue of an organizational culture more precisely be understood? The concept of communication can be analysed from different academic perspectives, but it is widely acknowledged that theories of meaning and understanding from philosophy of mind and language can be important resources in any conceptual analysis and thus also in analyses of organizational communication. This relevance of conceptions of meaning and shared language is first and foremost recognized in the abovementioned conceptions of organizational cultures as communicative practices but also in many other theoretical traditions that emphasize the importance of relational interaction in organizations [39, 44].

Within a general framework of philosophical analysis, I will in the following focus on four communication conditions—conditions that must be met for successful communication to happen. They focus, in turn, on the need to have attention, the importance of having a shared language, the need to avoid misinterpretation and the significance of understanding attitudes, values and preferences.

3.1 Attention

There is no hope of communication if a sender in a communicative process does not have the attention of the audience. Furthermore, communication has not succeeded if a message is not processed by an audience even though he or she observes the communicative act in question. This can happen, for instance, when an audience is so stressed or full of anxiety that a message does not really enter his or her consciousness [4, 5].

Having attention is particularly important in communication of action-guiding information. If such information is not received, the consequences—lack of action or nonintentional actions—can have dramatic negative consequences.

The importance of securing attention has a psychological dimension as well. If the argumentative basis for a decision does not reach the attention of an audience, there is an increased risk that the audience will fail to understand the rationale of the decision. For instance, changes in an organization can easily be experienced as negative by those who are affected by them if the justifications for the changes are not communicated properly [9]. Such lack of understanding of underlying reasons can cause a variety of negative consequences related to motivation, conflicts and (thereby) efficiency [20, 25].

3.2 Language

Having attention is no guarantee for communication. Consider a sender who aims to communicate something to an audience. The sender might have the attention of the audience—the audience might be able to observe the sender's communicative acts—but if they do not have a shared language, then the acts will not be interpreted as intended. Understood like this, having a shared language is also a necessary condition for communication. Communication breaks down if senders and audiences understand the language that is used—no matter what kind of language it is—in very different ways.

In philosophy of mind and language, there are various conceptions of what it means to share a language [6, 7, 37, 45, 46]. However, most theorists have, in one sense or another, tied this to exchange of concepts. As an illustration, consider as an everyday example a person who aims to communicate his belief that it is raining to another person. What is commonly defined as the propositional content of this belief is made up of the three concepts *it*, *is* and *raining*, and communication is successful if the audience associates the speech act with the same concepts as the sender, if the audience understands that the sender means *it is raining*. The sender and the audience need, in other words, to have a sufficiently similar understanding of the verbal or nonverbal expressions of meaning that are used [6, 46].

3.3 Associative misinterpretation

Together, having attention and having a shared language are still only necessary conditions for successful communication. The reason is that what is directly expressed in language is only the top of the iceberg in social interaction. In typical verbal or nonverbal dialogue, communicators ascribe to each other many beliefs and thoughts that are not literally expressed in words. Theoretically, the main reason is that in normal dialogue, communicators intend to be as economical as possible when they convey meaning. As Sperber and Wilson [47] observe:

> *When communicating humans automatically aim at maximal relevance, i.e. maximal cognitive effect for minimal processing effort. This is the single general factor which determines the course of human information processing.*

The point is that in ordinary communication we only say what we think we need in order to convey all that we want to communicate. We include the part of the communicative iceberg that is beneath the visible surface and hope, due to more or less contextual or conventional norms for interpretation, that the audience also gets the part of the message that is beneath the directly visible surface in the way we intend it to be understood [48].

An everyday example from an organization might be a situation involving a manager and an employee who talk about a job task. The manager asks 'Is it possible for you to look into this?' The employee interprets this as an informal request, but the manager, we can imagine, understands this differently. What he means is that he wants the employee to take responsibility for the task.

The lack of clarity about this might cause a misunderstanding and have negative consequences. We can imagine that the employee does nothing about the task—he thinks this is a viable option in the light of the managers' vague question—and that the manager after some time discovers that nothing has been done. He says to the employee: 'But I asked you to do this!' The employee gets frustrated. He thinks that the criticism is unfair in the light of what the manager actually asked him—he thinks that his interpretation of the question was valid.

In this kind of situation, it is always a good question if someone is to blame for the misunderstanding. Initially, one might think of this in the light of the idea of a social norm: If there is a common social norm for how an utterance should be interpreted, and if only one of the parties interpret a message in accordance with this norm, then the other party is, at least *prima facie*, to blame for the misunderstanding.

Here, the idea of a social norm can be understood broadly, as a norm in the whole language community. But it can also be understood more narrowly within a context or social group, as a way of interpreting what have been established as part of a culture [8, 43]. If there are many different contextual or group-related interpretative frameworks within an organization, then this can have a huge negative impact on organizational communication and, thereby, on organizational performance.

In many cases one might appeal to such broad or narrow norms in formal or informal analyses of misunderstandings—one can legitimately argue that a person's interpretation is non-standard compared to a relevant norm that it is normal to defer to. However, in some cases it is far from clear that there are any definite norms that should govern interpretation. In such cases it is often not justified to blame one or both communicators for the misunderstanding.

3.4 Relational communication

The abovementioned communication conditions focus on thoughts and beliefs—information that is expressed and interpreted. The final condition focuses on a remaining aspect of communication, what one might call the relational aspect of social interaction: In addition to beliefs and thoughts, senders attempt to convey attitudes, preferences and values, and communication is only successful if audiences interpret these mental states as they are expressed by senders.

The idea of similar interpretation is the same: A sender who intends to convey a mental state like an emotion, experience or attitude must be experienced in the intended way by the audience. The immediate consequence of this is that it is not how a person defines himself as someone who expresses a specific mental state that defines successful communication of this kind, but how he is experienced by his audience.

An example might be the attitude of empathy. Consider an employee in an organization who thinks of himself as empathetic in dialogue with a colleague. The employee's understanding of himself does not help for communicative purposes if the colleague does not experience him as empathetic. Or consider a manager who defines himself as a friendly person. There might be factors that cause his audience to experience him differently in a dialogue, for instance, the manager's body language. Then, for communicative purposes, he does not appear friendly to his audience. It is how the audience perceives him that determines how successful the communication is.

The same goes for a range of other non-conceptual mental states like values, interests and preferences. The way a sender intends to be understood must correspond to how the audience experiences him. Incongruent communication—communication in which there is an inconsistency between verbal and nonverbal language—causes uncertainty about intentions and negative interpretations [5]. Fundamentally, the significance of avoiding this kind of communication is connected to the need to clearly express positive attitudes in order to create a positive culture [49].

Together, the four communication conditions I have outlined can be understood as principles for communication that it is especially important what communicators think of. Communication as a process involves many aspects, and the process can be understood as a cycle: The audience needs to close the communicative loop, and in order to get a confirmation that a message has been received, senders need to get feedback from the audience [4, 5]. The four conditions above are core pitfalls that communicators easily can fall into when trying to secure two-way dialogue.

Turned around, the conditions can also be understood as conceptual resources. To each condition, there is a crucial question that any communicator can use as a mental checklist for evaluating the quality of social interaction: (1) Do I have the attention of my audience? (2) Do we have a shared language? (3) Do we interpret beliefs and thoughts that are not directly expressed in language in a sufficiently similar way? (4) Do the attitudes, values and preferences that we ascribe to each other correspond to what we intend to convey? These questions can be understood as methodological tools that can be implemented individually or collectively to sharpen communication practices.

4. Applications

The need to meet basic communication conditions is general and therefore also of crucial importance in organizations. Such conditions have not, however, been linked to organizational culture: In the academic literature, the question of how it is possible to change organizational culture by implementing communication principles has not received much attention.

The significance of this question is striking on personal levels. After all, and as Eisenberg and Riley ([43], p. 316) notes, 'the most significant information exchange among organizations has always occurred through personal flows'. However, the need to focus on communication as part of culture is recognized to be important on system levels as well. This has, in particular, been connected to the importance of creating communicative networks and especially to analyses of how such networks arise. Nevertheless, as Gailhurst [8] observes, the literature 'focuses much more on the creation of networks than their maintenance or dissolution ... [and] this reflects a serious shortcoming in current theoretical perspectives and empirical research'. This is the main reason why analyses of communicative cultures are so relevant. Such analyses can explore how formal and informal communication networks actually work.

This dependency between communication and the dynamics of cultures has been addressed in many ways. The important point for the present purposes is that both on individual and general levels, the four communication conditions above have striking implications for how it is possible to strengthen communicative organizational cultures. It is not difficult to understand how this is so.

4.1 A culture for efficient information exchange

Related to the abovementioned initial communication condition about attention, the most fundamental principle is to create a culture for involving all relevant persons in communication loops, so that relevant persons are included. Simply put, if action-guiding information does not reach the attention of relevant recipients, then members of the organization will not act as presupposed and thereby, at least typically, not in the best interest of the organization.

This point is of crucial importance on management levels and, more generally, in analyses of how communication channels should be designed throughout an organization [38]. It is, however, also significant for individuals, in the light of their personal responsibility for securing communication. In particular, it is an important individual responsibility to make sure that one does not become what Varey [27] labels an 'information dump'—a person who does not pass on information that should be passed on.

The amount of information that flows through organizations can be huge. A crucial communication principle is therefore to avoid creation of too much communicative noise—contextual disturbances or transmission of information that is not necessary or sufficiently important. Furthermore, it is imperative to clarify the most essential information. A thumb rule in communication theory is that if it is important to express a message in a clear and concise way, and if it is possible to state the message in such a way, then this should be done. This will normally be a matter of formulating the message in a language that expresses clear concepts that the communicators have a shared understanding of.

Another example of a principle related to attention that can be part of a common culture is the principle of giving summaries of information. This is something that typically should be done towards the end of a meeting or a formal talk like an appraisal interview. Furthermore, many dialogues involve a variety of sub-discourses, and it is not easy to identify the most important information for audiences. Controlling that information that has been received and digested can therefore be of crucial importance.

4.2 Creating a shared language

As noted above, barriers of meaning can create communicative gaps. In organizational theory, this has often been connected to barriers of meaning—inconsistent or even incommensurable ideas of what language means [13]. There are several ways in which such barriers occur in organizations, but many can be traced to roles, positions and opposing ideologies.

More fundamentally, the need to have a shared language can be tied to the significance of consensus. Brutal disagreement—conflicts—can have a variety of negative consequences [10, 44]. Many of the conflicts that arise in organizations are semantic conflicts. They are caused by inconsistent conceptions of what language expressions mean.

By creating a shared understanding of key concepts as part of a common culture, it is easier to avoid such conflicts. It is also important to remember that inconsistent conceptions of what expressions mean can be intimately tied to group thinking within an organization. Two good examples can be the expressions 'quality' and 'efficiency'. On management levels, interpretation of these expressions is often influenced by economic-administrative ideology: The word 'efficiency' is typically associated with economic performance and 'quality' with observable quality indicators. On first-line levels, on the other hand, 'efficiency' is less connected to resources, administrative thinking and economy, and 'quality' is often associated with professional standards—like the need to meet medical norms for sound patient treatment in organizations like hospitals.

If these kinds of inconsistent conceptions of what language mean are not uncovered, discussions about how it is possible to improve 'efficiency' and 'quality' can easily escalate into conflicts [13]. When this happens, the real root cause of the problem is that the parties in the conflicts have inconsistent understandings of the language that is used. These conflicts are, in reality, pseudo conflicts, and they can often be resolved in a simple way, by making the opposing parties aware of the fact that they understand language very differently.

4.3 Creating a culture for norms of interpretation

I emphasized that having a shared language is not sufficient for communication. When people interpret each other, they do so on the basis of vast and huge assumptions about the part of the message that is not directly expressed in language.

As noted above, the concept of a 'norm of interpretation' is highly relevant in analyses of poor and successful communication. Interpretation is always made on the basis of implicit or explicit norms of interpretation. Common concepts are, obviously, often used in interaction in organizations, and in such cases interpretation of utterances is crucially connected to 'outside' norms of public meaning. Some of these norms are explicit, others are more implicit. But no matter which of these categories relevant frameworks of meaning fall into, senders and audiences need to have learned the same 'external' norms—they need to share a sufficiently similar interpretive perspective.

It would be too demanding to expect that it is possible to create an organizational culture in which everyone has the same ideas of how utterances should be interpreted by relevant members of the organization. However, some potentially vague or disputed concepts can often have a central role in organizational discourses. By creating, as part of the organizational culture, a shared understanding of how these concepts should be interpreted, it is possible to prevent many unnecessary misunderstandings that can easily lead to conflict.

One example could be the concept of an information meeting. There is usually no fundamental *semantic* problem with this concept in organizational discourse: Communicators typically share a core conception of what a meeting is and what it means to give information in a meeting. Communicators can nevertheless have inconsistent ideas of how such a meeting should be arranged. Some might think that it is okay to have discussions in an information meeting. Others might think that such meetings should only involve one-way communication—typically from manager groups to employees affected by changes decided on management levels.

Disagreement about how successful a meeting has been can be caused by these kinds of inconsistent conceptions.

Another even more everyday example can be the word 'have' as in a message 'We have to do this' about a job task in a business. What does this mean? Some might interpret such an utterance literally and think that everything is at stake if the task is not done—that the business will go bankrupt (and a person who thinks this might react even more negatively if he thinks that it is impossible, within the given competence or resource situation, to get the job done). Others might think of the utterance in a weaker way—as a moral suggestion that the task in question merely should be done. Such misunderstandings can lead to different actions. The moral interpretation can easily lead someone to give priority to other tasks, and those who interpret the utterance in this way can end up in a conflict with those who interpret the utterance in the hard 'We *have* to do this' sense.

4.4 Creating a culture for communicating positive attitudes

In addition to the informative and action-guiding aspect of organizational communication, many theorists have recognised that manager-employee dialogue has 'softer' relational aspects and 'a human side' [31]. As Hargie observes, it has been extensively documented that:

> *... when we are suffering emotional difficulties, we remember how we are treated by managers and co-workers ... Concern shown for an employee, especially by a manager, is reciprocated in terms of increased attachment and loyalty to the corporation, with a resulting increase in effort ([12], p. 37).*

It is first and foremost personal motivation and organizational commitment that are affected by lack of intimacy [8, 21, 50]. And such attitudes, it has been recognised, are grounded in well-functioning relations with managers. It has been extensively documented that employees appreciate communicative managers.

To a large extent, this is a question of being informative and communicating positive attitudes like concern, care and empathy when this is needed. As noted above, to really communicate, an attitude involves more than expressing it. It has to be experienced in the intended way by the audience in the communicative process.

There is, of course, many things individual members of an organization can do in order to contribute in creating a culture in which practices of communicating positive attitudes are recognized as important. Furthermore, some persons are, more often than others, disposed to interpret the world through a negative filter, and by understanding the importance of having a less negative perspective, individuals can improve their relations to others [44, 49].

On system levels, collective learning about the importance of good relations can have individual implications so that the organizational culture as a whole is improved. Such initiatives can, to a large extent, use resources from positive psychology and empirical studies, models and theories about job engagement and motivational behaviour from organizational theory. The potential of such collective learning has, in particular, been connected to human resource management. Many studies have shown that there is a correlation between inspiring management and employee motivation and, in turn, between motivation and organizational performance [15, 20].

Again, the point is that when there is a collective focus on this, then positive changes become part of a cultural improvement. It concerns how something is done generally. By making the importance of relational aspects of interaction part of a shared consciousness—as 'this is how we do it'—then the shared focus will shape practices in a positive way.

Much more could be said about the importance of shared implementation of communication practices. However, doing that would fall outside the limits of this article. The aim has been of a more general character: I have argued that focusing on issues related to communication is important for building organizational culture. The communication principles I have focused on are especially important for the purpose of reaching this goal, so there is a special incentive for implementing on them within the organization. But the importance of establishing a communicative culture is more general.

5. Conclusion

In the literature on organization theory, the dependency between organizational communication, culture and performance has been recognized and explored in many ways. Focusing on this dependency falls under what Gailhurst [8] calls a dialogue perspective on organizational communication generally and on manager-employee communication in particular:

> *An individualistic focus produces the tendency to see the leader's communication in monologic and transmission terms. A system focus emphasizes meaning as a social construction through leader-constituent dialogue.*

Focusing on organizational culture as a communicative practice falls under the latter focus and has been tied to the correlation between good 'two-way' dialogue and organizational performance. That there is this kind of correlation and that it is important have been recognized in the literature. However, there have not been many studies that have contributed to explaining how this should be understood in more detail.

The aim of this article has been to contribute to this 'how' issue. I have done this by introducing key concepts from communication theory and explained how the concepts are relevant for understanding and improving culture. A communicative organizational culture, I have argued, can be improved by focusing on attention, language, interpretation and attitudes. In each way these concepts give substance to the idea of a relational culture—how it can be created, maintained and, most importantly, developed.

Obviously, much more could be said about communication and culture. In this sense an important aim of this chapter has been to set a general agenda: Good communication is crucial for establishing a good culture. Consequently, in order to get a sufficiently rich focus on the significance of organizational culture, future theoretical and empirical research cannot ignore organizational dialogue as a research area. Furthermore, research should not only explore how communication theory is relevant for understanding organizational culture. There is also a need for scientific models and principles that can be used in a normative sense to improve culture.

Author details

Halvor Nordby
Faculty of Health and Social Work, Inland Norway University of Applied Sciences, Lillehammer, Norway

*Address all correspondence to: halvor.nordby@inn.no

References

[1] Benhabib S. Critique, Norm, and Utopia: A Study of the Foundations of Critical Theory. New York: Columbia University Press; 1986

[2] Gadamer HG. Truth and Method. New York: Seabury Press; 1975

[3] Habermas J. The Theory of Communicative Action. London: Beacon Press; 1981

[4] Littlejohn S, Foss K. Theories of Human Communication. Belmont, CA: Wadsworth publishing; 2007

[5] Wood J. Interpersonal Communication. Belmont, CA: Wadsworth Publishing; 2009

[6] Burge T. Individualism and the mental. Midwest Studies in Philosophy. 1979;**4**:73-122

[7] Cappelen H, Lepore E. Insensitive Semantics. Oxford: Blackwell; 2005

[8] Gailhurst G. Dualisms in leadership research. In: Jablin F, Putnam L, editors. The New Handbook of Organizational Communication. London: Sage Publications; 2001. pp. 379-440

[9] Kotter J. Leading Change. Boston, Massachusetts: Harvard Business Review Press; 2012

[10] Roche W, Teague P, Colvin J. The Oxford Handbook of Conflict Management in Organizations. Oxford: Oxford University Press; 2014

[11] Brønn C, van Ruler B, Vercic D. Organizations, communication and management. In: Brønn P, Berg R, editors. Corporate Communication. Oslo: Gyldendal Akademisk; 2005. pp. 59-79

[12] Hargie O. Managing your communications: A key determinant of organizational success. In: Karlsdottir R, editor. Læring, Kommunikasjon og Ledelse i Organisasjoner. Trondheim: Tapir Akademisk Forlag; 2007. pp. 23-45

[13] Nordby H. Management communication in leadership relations. A philosophical model of understanding and contextual agreement. Philosophy of Management. 2014;**13**(2):75-100

[14] Harigopal K. Organizational Stress: A Study of Role Conflicts. Hyderabad: Universities Press; 1995

[15] Truss C, Alfes K, Delbridge R, Shantz A, Soane E. Employee Engagement in Theory and Practice. London: Routledge; 2014

[16] Choo CW. The Knowing Organization. 2th ed. Oxford: Oxford University Press; 2006

[17] Smith L, Mounter P. Effective Internal Communication. London: Kogan Page Limited; 2008

[18] Tompkins PK, Wanca-Thibault M. Organizational communication: Prelude and prospects. In: Jablin F, Putnam L, editors. The New Handbook of Organizational Communication (Preface). London: Sage Publications; 2001

[19] Downs CW, Clampitt PG, Pfeiffer AL. Communication and organizational outcomes. In: Goldhaber G, Barnett G, editors. Handbook of Organizational Communication. Norwood, NJ: Ablex; 1988. pp. 171-211

[20] Bakker AB, Leiter MP. Work Engagement. Hove and New York: Psychology Press; 2010

[21] Hargie O, Tourish D. Assessing the effectiveness of communication in organizations. Health Services Management Research. 1993;**6**:276-285

[22] Weick KE. Sensemaking in Organizations. Thousand Oaks, CA: Sage Publications; 1995

[23] Willmott H. Organization theory as a critical science. In: Tsoukas H, Knudsen C, editors. The Oxford Handbook of Organizational Theory. Oxford: Oxford University Press; 2003. pp. 88-113

[24] Gagne M. The Oxford Handbook of Work Engagement, Motivation and Self-Determination. Oxford: Oxford University Press; 2014

[25] Wentland D. Organizational Performance in a Nutshell. Charlotte, North Carolina: Information Age Publishing; 2009

[26] Varey R. A critical review of conceptions of communication evident in contemporary business and management literature. Journal of Communication Management. 1993;**4**:328-3s40

[27] Varey R. Responsive and responsible communication practices: A pluralist perspective. In: Brønn P, Berg R, editors. Corporate Communication. Oslo: Gyldendal Akademisk; 2005. pp. 83-101

[28] Nagel T. The View from Nowhere. Oxford: Oxford University Press; 1986

[29] Rasmussen D. Reading Habermas. London: Blackwell; 1990

[30] Jablin F, Sias P. Communication competence. In: Jablin F, Putnam L, editors. The New Handbook of Organizational Communication. London: Sage Publications; 2001. pp. 819-865

[31] Ivancevich J. Human Resource Management. In: New York. McGraw-Hill: Irwin; 2006

[32] Mathis R, Jackson J. Human Resource Management. Andover: Cengage Learning; 2010

[33] Mueller-Vollmer K. The Hermeneutics Reader. New York: Continuum; 1985

[34] Schmidt D. Gadamer. In: Critchley S, Schroeder W, editors. A Companion to Continental Philosophy. Oxford: Blackwell; 1999. pp. 60-75

[35] Dancy J. Introduction to Contemporary Epistemology. Oxford: Wiley-Blackwell; 1991

[36] Bermudez J. Philosophy of Psychology. London: Routledge; 2005

[37] Peacocke C. A Study of Concepts. Cambridge/Mass: MIT Press; 1992

[38] Johnson D. Managing Knowledge Networks. Cambridge: Cambridge University Press; 2009

[39] Yukl G. Leadership in Organizations. Upper Saddle River, New Jersey: Pearson; 2013

[40] Schein E. Understanding Organizational Culture. San Francisco, California: Jossey-Bass; 2010

[41] Cameron K, Quinn R. Diagnosing and Changing Organizational Culture. San Francisco, California: Jossey-Bass; 2011

[42] Alvesson M. Understanding organizational culture. London: Sage publications; 2012

[43] Eisenberg E, Riley P. Organizational culture. In: Jablin M, Putnam L, editors. The New Handbook of Organizational Culture. London: Sage publications; 2001

[44] Arnold J, Randall R. Work Psychology. Essex: Pearson Education Limited; 2010

[45] Carston R. Thoughts and Utterances. Oxford: Blackwell; 2002

[46] Nordby H. Concept possession and incorrect understanding. Philosophical Explorations. 2004;**7**:55-71

[47] Sperber D, Wilson D. Loose talk. Proceedings of the Aristotelian Society. 1986;**86**:153-171

[48] Sperber D, Wilson D. Relevance: Communication and Cognition. Oxford: Blackwell; 2005

[49] Eagly A, Chaiken S. The Psychology of Attitudes. Fort Worth, Texas: Harcourt Brace Jovanovich; 1993

[50] Quinn R et al. Becoming a Master Manager: A Competing Values Approach. Hoboken, NJ: Wiley; 2007

Chapter 8

Learning Culture as the Enabler of Business Transformation

Nopriadi Saputra and Ismiriati Nasip

Abstract

Business organizations experience not only episodic but also continuous and disruptive changes. Those changes make the organization need not only transitional and developmental but also transformational initiatives. Based on business transformational experience in many prominent companies, organizational culture was one of eight factors that make transformation fail. Organizational culture plays a strategic role in business transformations and management. It can be an asset or liability for business transformation. The development of organizational culture should not only impact on work engagement but also learning agility of people in the organization. Based on the impact, organizational culture can be differentiated from the hierarchal-centralistic culture and the learning culture. By using the concept of culture map, learning culture is mapped and reflected into eight dimensions: communicating, evaluating, persuading, leading, deciding, trusting, disagreeing, and scheduling. By mapping the culture gap of the current condition, management practitioner has a road map for developing the learning culture.

Keywords: business agility, learning culture, culture map

1. Introduction

The discovery and utilization of technology have brought fundamental and revolutionary changes in the world. These changes have enabled companies to have better opportunities in creating and delivering value to their customers. The discovery and utilization of mechanization, electricity, and automation technology have led to Industry 1.0, Industry 2.0, and Industry 3.0. These technologies have enabled companies to conduct mass production simultaneously non-stop without interruption 24 hours a day, 7 days a week [1]. The latest developments of the Internet and the utilization of digital technologies or cyber-physical systems in doing business have also led the world to Industry 4.0.

Digital technology enables companies to collaborate with different parties wherever and whenever around the world in achieving their sustainable business growth [1]. In addition to making it easy to collaborate and innovate, digital technology also brings companies into the VUCA World—a world which makes business become more volatile, more uncertain, more complex, and more ambiguous [2–4]. The VUCA world causes the convergence of various defined industries. One consequence of the VUCA world is that the life expectation of companies has decreased. In 1958, average of a company's life expectation that was listed in the Standard and Poor's 500 was 61 years. This life expectation had shrunk to 25 years in 1980 and 18 years in 2012. It is even predicted that a company's life expectation is going to shrink to 10 years in 2020 [5].

IntechOpen

2. Business agility and transformational initiative

That is why one of the challenges companies face today is the business sustainability. Many companies, especially large companies that become the market leaders, must be able to adapt quickly by developing business agility [6–9]. Business agility is the ability of a company to anticipate and utilize business opportunities and to avoid the negative consequences of changes quickly, flexibly, and decisively [10]. Meanwhile, business agility is defined as the organizational capability to innovate through collaboration and to anticipate business challenges and opportunities before these changes occur [7].

There are three types of initiatives that companies can take in adapting to business environment changes. They are developmental, transitional, and transformational initiatives [11]. Building and developing business flexibility is a transformational initiative because it requires fundamental change in culture, behavior, and mentality of people in the organization as a whole. The initiative has uncertainty and runs a high risk of failure. The initiative also requires a lot of resources and the effectiveness of the transformational initiative will have a major impact on the company's sustainability.

From the perspective of organizational development (OD), the development of business agility requires change management capability in open system context. It is more than individual or group dynamic context. The transformational initiative is implemented in the context of the organization as an open system where the business is influenced by the environment and consists of various and interacting subsystems. In the open systems context, transformational initiatives can be viewed in four main subsystems. They are organizational goals and values, management capability, psychological and technical perspective [12]. This chapter elaborates the development of business agility as a transformational initiative that focused on the organizational goals and values subsystem only.

Based on research in more than 100 prominent companies, it is discovered that there are eight reasons why a transformation fails. Those factors are: (1) easy to compromise with circumstances, (2) not building coalitions that are strong enough to support the transformation, (3) underestimating the power of vision, (4) not communicating the vision of transformation intensively, (5) having obstacles hindering the vision of transformation, (6) no transformation to short-term success of transformation, (7) explain the success of information transformation too quickly, and (8) make transformation was not part of the corporate culture [13]. Because corporate culture is an important factor in determining the success of a transformation, this chapter attempts to further evaluate transformation initiatives to build business agility from the perspective of corporate culture.

3. Corporate culture as the proposed approach

Corporate culture can be defined as a system of ideas that is developed dynamically in a social system called business organization [14], contains a set of defined attitudes, values, behaviors, and expectations [15], gained through shared experiences from external adaptation and internal integration processes [16], then agreed as the way of thinking, perceiving, and responding to solve problems [17] and become distinctive identity which distinguish themselves from other companies or organizations [18].

Corporate culture is an organizational capability that is source of sustainable competitive advantage (SCA), as long as corporate culture is well managed and developed by company; produce a positive effect on business performance; difficult for other companies to imitate; and only a few companies developed it [19]. An empirical research has been conducted on eight pairs of companies from eight different industries. Each pair consists of a successful company and a company with financial difficulties in the same industry. The research measured and tested every aspect and how important are the differences between the two groups of companies when doing business. The research concluded that successful companies have proven significantly better at six capabilities: managing markets; managing products; managing resources; managing operational systems; managing managerial systems; and managing corporate culture. Organizational capability in managing corporate culture is an essential factor and differentiator that distinguishes successful companies and companies with financial difficulties [20].

Previous empirical research has also shown that corporate culture has a positive and significant impact on an organization's ability to adapt, innovate, be agile, and dare to take risks in a turbulent business environment [21–27]. Corporate culture influences the strategic orientation and financial performance of the company [21]. In the context of corporate globalization, corporate culture plays an important role in influencing corporate capacity to take risks. Cultural values that prevent uncertainty and harmony have negative effects, while cultural values that have individualism have a positive effect on the company's ability to take risk [22].

Learning culture has a positive and significant impact on the organizational flexibility in the port industry [23]. A flexibility-oriented culture or development culture has a positive and significant impact on adaptability and the ability to innovate [24]. Corporate culture that is focused on novelty has a positive and significant impact on the strategic flexibility of the company. Although a business culture focused on efficiency has no influence on strategic agility [25], corporate culture that is hierarchical—such as bureaucratic, strict with the rules and one directional from top to bottom, weakens the effect of absorbency on organizational agility [26]. Related to transformational initiatives to build business agility, the business culture can be an enabler as well as a block for the company in dealing with changes. A company cannot create a corporate culture overnight, nor can it change a corporate culture overnight. But we can identify which behaviors are relevant and important for developing business agility and then we can nurture them in the context of corporate culture in the whole organization [27].

4. Learning culture as a part of corporate culture

Company as an organization that deals with dynamic changes needs adaptive capability. The adaptive capability is developed by learning activities individually, collectively, and organizationally. Those learning activities are not sporadic and temporary, but they must be conducted systematically and continuously.

Learning has become a culture with learning activities in the company displaying four indicators [16]. First is the width indicator. Learning activity is not only carried out by one or several people but by most people in the company. They come from various functions and various layers of the organization. Second is the depth indicator. Learning activity is not an impulsive or temporary behavior, but it has become a habitual behavior or even become a permanent character. Third is the integration indicator. Learning activity has been integrated with the main systems within the company. Fourth is the structural stability indicator. Learning activity will be conducted continuously. No matter who is the top executive of the company, no matter who comes in and goes out the company, learning activity is continuously conducted in the whole company.

Learning culture is a derivative concept of corporate culture in management and it comes from the culture concept in sociology. Culture concept refers to AGIL scheme from the theory of action [28]. AGIL scheme explains that a social system in order to become sustainable requires four main functions to be considered: first, Adaptation—how the resources needed by the social system can be fulfilled; second, Goal attainment—how the social system collectively sets a common goal and makes it happen; third Integration—how the social system maintains solidity and coordinates to achieve common goals; fourth, Latency—how the social system creates, maintains, and passes on relevant values to new members who come later. Organizational culture is part of the latency function, which is how organizations create, maintain, and pass down relevant value systems for the sustainability and future progress of the company to all existing and new employees.

In the early 1980s, two books were published that sparked the development concept of corporate culture. Those books are *In Search of Excellence* [29] which concludes that the difference between high- and low-performing companies is that they have a strong culture and *Corporate Culture* [30] which suggests that organizational performance can be improved by strengthening the shared values that are believed by whole employees in their daily business practices.

The concept of learning culture also refers to organizational culture theory [31], organizational learning theory [32], and learning organization [33]. Organizational culture theory explains several things. First, organizational culture is an adaptive feature of organizations that has an influence on organizational effectiveness. Second, company founders and top leaders are very influential in instilling values into organizational culture. Third, organizational culture reflects collective learning about what works/does not work for dealing with organizational challenges. Fifth, organizational culture is composed of artifacts, values, and basic assumptions used by companies in carrying out business practices [31].

Whereas organizational learning theory [32] explains that in facing a changing environment, organizations are encouraged to create mechanisms to produce effective actions and then be taught to all organizations so that organizational goals can be realized. There are two types of learning, namely: (1) single-loop learning—which occurs when errors are detected and corrected but do not make changes in principle, and (2) double-loop learning—which occurs when correcting errors and requires changes in principle [34]. This organizational learning theory continues to grow and then becomes the basis for the concept of learning organization [33].

Learning organization [33] explains that culture is a pattern of basic assumptions learned by groups or organizations to overcome problems in terms of external adaptation and internal integration. This is considered a valid way and is taught to new members of the organization as a perspective for overcoming future challenges. In developing a company into a learning organization, there are five subsystems that must support one another. Those are learning process, organization, employees, knowledge, and technology. The learning process subsystem must get attention, especially on three things: first, the level of learning that includes individuals, teams, and organizations; second, the type of learning that are anticipative, adaptive, and/or action learning; third, learning skills, which consist of systemic thinking, mental models, personal mastery, independent learning, and dialogic processes [33].

The previous researchers have their own definitions and views about learning culture. Organizational learning culture is an organizational culture that is directed to encourage and facilitate employees in doing organizational learning, both individual and group learning, and the learning contributes to organizational development, performance, and success [35]. Learning culture has the capacity for integrating people and structures to move organizations toward learning and sustainable change [36]. Learning culture is viewed as values, beliefs, and assumptions that encourage the realization of collective learning in the whole organizations [37].

Learning culture from organizational culture, has a difference or distinctiveness than other organizational culture such as work culture, service culture, or mutual culture. Learning culture makes learning as core value of the company. Learning culture is oriented to the development of human capabilities. Learning culture concerns all stakeholders, stimulates experimentation, and fosters responsible for risk attitude. Learning culture builds a willingness and openness to learn from mistakes and promotes open and intensive communication to work together, interdependence, and knowledge sharing.

5. Impact on work engagement and learning agility

The previous study has proven that corporate culture has positive and significant impact on work engagement. Employees who have a mindset, value system, and habits that are relevant to the corporate culture will be encouraged to stay engaged to the company.

Some concepts that related to corporate culture that have been proven empirically to be antecedents of work engagement are organizational culture [38–41], psycho-social safety climate [42], psychological climate [43, 44], supportive organizational culture [45], service culture [46], safety culture [47], and ethical culture [48].

Several studies have proven empirically that culture has a significant effect on work engagement. Learning culture has a positive and significant effect on organizational commitment and job satisfaction [49]. Organizational learning culture has a positive and significant effect on job satisfaction and customer satisfaction. While organizational commitment and job satisfaction are also part of work engagement. As a consequence of this, both studies have indirectly proven that there is a cultural influence on work engagement [23].

Empirical study on 394 hospitality professionals in the United States have proved empirically that psychological climate is an antecedent of work attachment as well as moderating variables on the effect of core self-evaluation on work attachment. Psychological climate covers aspects of customer orientation, internal services, managerial support, as well as information and communication. Meanwhile, the psychological climate has a close concept with corporate culture [44].

Organizational learning culture has a positive and significant influence on affective commitment and organizational citizenship behavior, and intention to exit. Affective commitment and intention to exit are also part of work engagement [50]. Workplace ethical culture through mediation from perceived ethical leadership has a significantly positive effect on work engagement in the whole dimensions—vigor, dedication, and absorption [51].

A multi-level longitudinal research on 134 employees in Malaysia also proved that hierarchical culture and empowering leadership significantly impact on work engagement [52]. But contrary to empirical study by Collier, Fitzpatrick, Siedlecki, and Dolansky, it has proved oppositely that employee engagement actually has a positive and significant effect on the application of safety culture by nurses from 25 ICUs in United States hospitals. Work engagement is the antecedent of the culture, not the culture is an antecedent of attachment [53].

In addition, the learning culture also has a positive and significant impact on learning agility of the employees. Learning culture will encourage the employees continuously to carry out learning activities individually, collectively, and organizationally in their daily routine activity. In the long term, it will build and develop learning agility. Learning agility is different from learning ability.

Learning agility is defined as the individual ability to be flexible and speedy in utilizing experiences to deal with complex and new situations. Learning agility is reflected in four dimensions: (1) mental agility is the willingness to make difficulties, failures, and mistakes as a vehicle for learning; (2) change agility is enthusiasm in utilizing the changes that occur as a vehicle for learning; (3) result agility is the ability to focus on achievement despite being in a complex condition for a long period; and (4) people agility is the ability to learn from the experiences of others and collaborate with others in achieving superior performance.

Several studies have empirically proven the impact of corporate culture on learning. Organizational learning culture together with transformational leadership has a significant positive impact on organizational learning which then impacts the learning performance of the agricultural faculty [54]. Learning culture had a positive and significant effect on learning achievement of 209 nursing students experimentally in three different learning environments [55]. Organizational learning culture has a positive and significant impact on individual capabilities, especially in exploration, exploitation, and individual creativity [56].

Study on 475 logistics service provider units in the United States has proven that learning culture and knowledge management have a positive and significant effect on human capital [57]. Meanwhile, human capital is knowledge, skills, and abilities obtained and accumulated through various learning processes such as training, development, education, and experiential learning [58]. Islamic work ethics has a positive and significant effect on adaptive performance mediated by innovative work behavior and moderated by ethical leadership through conducting research on 257 hospitality industry employees in Pakistan. This confirms that the work culture based on Islamic ethics influences the ability to learn, especially in innovation [59]. Empirical study on 123 lecturers from the Top 100 MBAs in India and proved that organizational learning culture had a significant and positive effect on motivation to transfer training, which was negatively moderated by resistance to change and moderated moderately positive by coaching performance [60].

Learning culture as a corporate culture has been proven from the many studies which apparently not only impact on work engagement, but also impact on learning agility of their employees. Learning culture will encourage employees not only to be engaged with the company for long period, but also endorse employees to adapt continuous and disruptive changes through their flexibility and speed in learning.

6. Transforming corporate culture into learning culture

Based on its impact on work engagement and learning agility, corporate culture can be grouped into three categories: No Impact, Single Impact, and Double Impact. No impact category is a corporate culture that has no impact or only has a low impact on work engagement and learning agility. We call this corporate culture a hierarchical-centralistic culture. Single impact category is a company culture that impacts on learning agility only or on work engagement only. This category can make employees engaged-but-not-adaptive or adaptive-but-not-engaged. The third category is the double impact culture. That is learning culture. Corporate culture that impacts both work engagement and learning agility. The learning culture makes employees engaged and adaptive to the business changes (**Figure 1**).

A hierarchical-centralistic culture makes teams or organizations less dynamic. Because subordinates who deal directly with operational situations on the ground

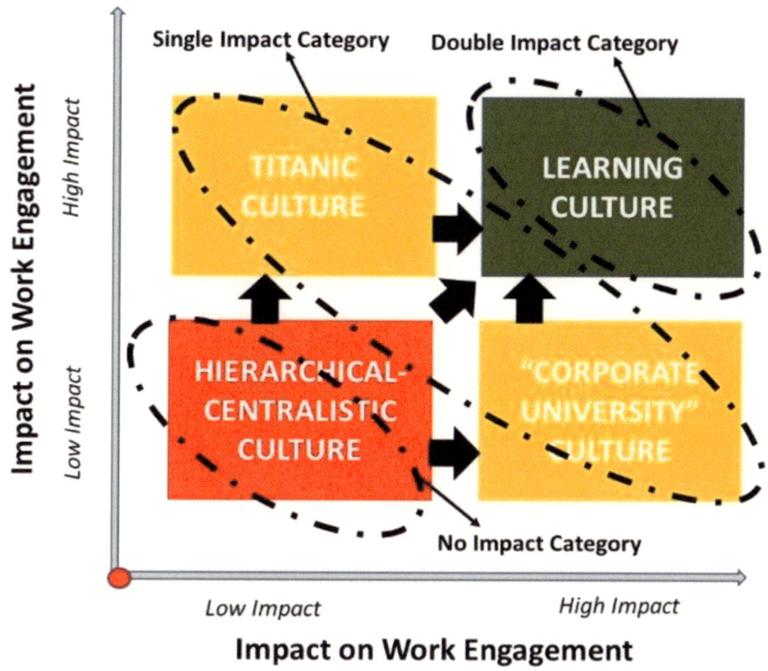

Figure 1.
Corporate culture category.

do not have the freedom to think and decide which actions will be the best to. Meanwhile superiors do not have enough information to make quick and right decisions. As a result, companies experience delays as well as rigidity in the face of a constantly changing environment. Besides that, in a hierarchical-centralistic culture, all problems that arise naturally become the authority to think and make decisions. Employees only accept decisions and carry out task orders.

Therefore, the corporate culture should be transformed from a hierarchical-centralistic culture to a learning culture. It is important for us to elaborate what the essential differences between hierarchical-centralistic and learning culture are. By using the culture map, the hierarchical-centralistic culture has eight tendencies:

1. Hierarchical: In hierarchical-centralistic culture, there is a psychological distance or power distance between superiors and subordinates. Superiors treat subordinates inferior so that subordinates are not free enough to express their thoughts to superiors. Then superiors tend to be closed to the thoughts of subordinates.

2. Top-down: In a hierarchical-centralistic culture, decisions are made entirely by superiors. Subordinates are only involved in the process of execution or implementation.

3. Indirect negative feedback: In hierarchical-centralistic culture, there is often a sense of reluctance to provide negative feedback to the work team, especially to superiors, for fear of offending the person.

4. High context: Hierarchical-centralistic culture in communication really cares about the right ways to convey thoughts, rather than the true intentions and goals.

5. Relationship based: In trusting, other people are more inclined based on relationships that are built. It is hard to trust people who are just known or did not have a good relationship before.

6. Avoid confrontation: In hierarchical-centralistic culture, people always avoid arguing to achieve objective and factual thinking.

7. Principle first: In hierarchical-centralistic culture, persuading others is done by presenting the underlying philosophical principles.

8. Linear time: In hierarchical-centralistic culture, activities are arranged sequentially or one by one, completing one thing first, then continuing to other things next (**Figure 2**).

Meanwhile, the learning culture that wants to be developed companies for enabling business agility development. It has the opposite tendency compared to the hierarchical-centralized culture:

1. Egalitarian: In learning culture, relationship between superiors and subordinates should be equal. Power distance is strived to be as minimal as possible. This will make it easier for subordinates to express their ideas and superiors are open to learning from subordinates.

2. Consensual: In learning culture, decisions made should be the result of a mutual agreement between the supervisor who is responsible for the results and subordinates who are responsible for the process.

3. Direct negative feedback: In learning culture, everyone has freedom to convey negative feedback to anyone. The underlying spirit is to achieve the common good (collaborative driven), not to bring down other parties (competitive driven).

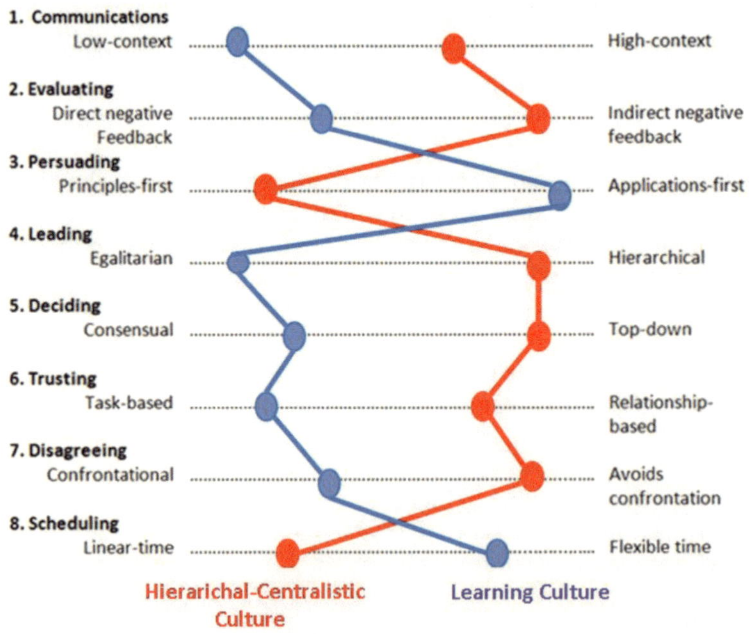

Figure 2.
Hierarchical-centralistic vs. learning culture.

4. Low context: In learning culture, communication should pay more attention to the content of messages rather than the way they are delivered. It cares more about what is conveyed than who delivers it.

5. Task-based: In learning culture, persons should be trusted based on their ability to complete tasks well, not based on how good the relationship is. Thus, even new people who join the team can be quickly given the opportunity to get involved in the problem-solving effort.

6. Confrontation: In learning culture, confrontation or argumentation is the best way to achieve objective and factual thinking.

7. Application first: In learning culture, others are persuaded based on aspects of application. How well the new concepts, ideas, or findings can be applied and provide the expected results. It is not based on philosophical concepts that become the background.

8. Flexible time: In learning culture; activities are scheduled flexibly. It is more goal-oriented and accommodates lots of dynamic changes or developments. More activities are carried out in parallel rather than just serially.

By understanding the culture map that explains the differences in characteristics between hierarchical-centralistic and learning culture, it makes it easy for us to carry out transformational initiative in developing corporate culture. By using cultural elements, the set of behaviors of employees can be directed more in line with what is expected by learning culture. It is especially the behaviors in communicating, evaluating, persuading, leading, deciding, trusting, disagreeing, and scheduling.

7. Conclusion

Technological developments have brought the companies into industrial revolution 4.0 and VUCA world, which makes companies experience continuous and disruptive changes intensively. For protecting their sustainable growth, it is imperative for companies to take transformational initiative. Transformational initiative is directed to develop business agility as the organizational adaptive capability. In implementing transformational initiative, corporate culture often becomes an obstacle or a blocker rather than an enabler. Directing corporate culture into learning culture is one of the recommended efforts.

Learning culture is a corporate culture that encourages learning activities carried out systematically and continuously on individuals, teams, and organization scope. The learning culture that is developed will have an impact on work engagement and also learning agility of employees throughout the company. Culture map can be used as compass to help the management in directing corporate culture into learning culture.

Author details

Nopriadi Saputra* and Ismiriati Nasip
Bina Nusantara University, Jakarta, Indonesia

*Address all correspondence to: nopriadi.saputra@binus.ac.id

References

[1] Schwab K. The Fourth Industrial Revolution: What it means and how to respond. World Economic Forum; 2016

[2] Bawany S. Leading in a VUCA business environment. Leadership Excellence Essentials. 2016;7:39-40

[3] Johansen B. Leaders Make the Future: Ten New Leadership Skills for an Uncertain World (First Edit). Bernett-Koehler Publishers, Inc.; 2009

[4] Mack O, Khare A, Kramer A, Burgatz T. Perspectives on a VUCA world. In: Managing in a VUCA World. 2016. pp. 3-19

[5] Glauner F. Future Viability, Business Models and Values; 2016

[6] Evans ND. Business Agility: Strategies for Gaining Competitive Advantage through Mobile Business Solutions. Prentice Hall; 2002

[7] Heisterberg R, Verma A. Creating Business Agility: How Convergence of Cloud, Social, Mobile, Video and Big Data Enables Competitive Advantage. Hoboken, New Jersey: John Wiley & Son, Inc.; 2014

[8] Hugos MH. Business Agility: Sustainable Prosperity in a Relentlessly Competitive World (Microsoft Executive Leadership Series); 2009

[9] McCann J, Selsky J, Lee J. Building agility, resilience and performance in turbulent environments. People and Strategy. 2009;**32**(3):44-51

[10] McCann J, Selsky J. Mastering Turbulence: The Essential Capabilities of Agile and Resilient Individuals, Teams and Organizations. London: Jossey-Bass; 2012

[11] Anderson D, Anderson LA. Beyond Change Management: How to Achieve Breakthrough Results through Conscious Change Leadership. Second ed. Pfeiffer; 2010

[12] Al-Haddad S, Kotnour T. Integrating the organizational change literature: A model for successful change. Journal of Organizational Change Management. 2015;**28**(2):234-262

[13] Kotter JP. Leading change: Why transformation efforts fail. Harvard Business Review. 1995:59-67

[14] Allaire Y, Firsirotu ME. Theories of organizational culture. Organization Studies. 1984

[15] Greenberg J, Baron RA. Behavior in Organizations: Understanding and Managing the Human Side of Work: Color Transparencies. Prentice Hall; 1997

[16] Schein EH. Organizational Culture and Leadership. 4th ed. San Francisco: Jossey-Bass; 2010

[17] Ahmed PK, Loh AYE, Zairi M. Cultures for continuous improvement and learning. Total Quality Management. 1999;**10**(4-5):426-434. DOI: 10.1080/0954412997361

[18] Hofstede G, Hofstede GJ, Minkoy M. Cultures and Organizations—Software of the Mind. Cultures and Organizations (Revised). McGraw-Hill; 2010

[19] Barney JB. Organizational culture: Can it be a source of sustained competitive advantage? Academy of Management Review. 1986;**11**(3):656-665

[20] Flamholtz E, Hua W. Searching for competitive advantage in the black box. European Management Journal. 2003;**21**(2):222-236. DOI: 10.1016/S0263-2373(03)00017-3

[21] Han HS. The relationship among corporate culture, strategic orientation, and financial performance. Cornell Hospitality Quarterly. 2012;**53**(3):207-219

[22] Li K, Griffin D, Yue H, Zhao L. How does culture influence corporate risk-taking? Journal of Corporate Finance. 2013;**23**:1-22

[23] Pantouvakis A, Bouranta N. Agility, organisational learning culture and relationship quality in the port sector. Total Quality Management & Business Excellence. 2017;**28**:366-378

[24] Adriansyah A, Afiff AZ. Organizational culture, absorptive capacity, innovation performance and competitive advantage: An Integrated Assessment in Indonesian Banking Industry. The South East Asian Journal of Management. 2015

[25] Hock M, Clauss T, Schulz E. The impact of organizational culture on a firm's capability to innovate the business model. R and D Management. 2016;**46**(3):433-450

[26] Felipe CM, Roldan JL, Leal-Rodriquez AL. An explanatory and predictive model for organizational agility. Journal of Business Research. 2016;**69**(10):4624-4631

[27] Perkin N, Abraham P. Building the Agile Business through Digital Transformation. Kogan Page; 2017

[28] Parsons T, Shils EA. Values and value orientations in the theory of action. In: Toward a General Theory of Action. Vol. 5. 1951. pp. 388-433

[29] Peters T, Waterman RH. In Search of Excellence: Lessons from America's Best-run Companies; 1982

[30] Deal TE, Kennedy AA. Corporate Cultures: The Rites and Rituals of Organizational Life. Addison-Wesley; 1982

[31] Schein EH. Organizational Culture: A Dynamic Model; 1983

[32] Argyris C, Schön DA. Organizational Learning: A Theory of Action Perspective. Addison-Wesley Publishing Company; 1978

[33] Marquardt MJ. Building the Learning Organization: A Systems Approach to Quantum Improvement and Global Success; 1996

[34] Smith KG, Hitt MA. Great Minds in Management—The Process of Theory Development. Oxford University Press; 2005

[35] Rebelo TM, Gomes AD. Conditioning factors of an organizational learning culture. Journal of Workplace Learning. 2011;**23**(3):173-194

[36] Egan TM, Yang B, Bartlett KR. The effects of organizational learning culture and job satisfaction on motivation to transfer learning and turnover intention. Human Resource Development Quarterly. 2004;**15**(3):279-301

[37] Sorakraikitikul M, Siengthai S. Organizational learning culture and workplace spirituality. The Learning Organization. 2014;**21**(3):175-192

[38] Alarcon G, Lyons JB, Tartaglia F. Understanding predictors of engagement within the military. Military Psychology. 2010;**22**(3):301-310

[39] Arifin F, Troena EA, Djumahir. Organizational culture, transformational leadership, work engagement and teacher's performance: Test of a model. International Journal of Educational Research. 2014;**2**(1):1-14

[40] MacIntosh EW, Doherty A. The influence of organizational culture on job satisfaction and intention to leave. Sport Management Review. 2010;**13**(2):106-117

[41] Naidoo P, Martins N. Investigating the relationship between organisational culture and work engagement. Problems and Perspectives in Management. 2014;**12**(4):432-440

[42] Dollard MF, Bakker AB. Psychosocial safety climate as a precursor to conducive work environments, psychological health problems, and employee engagement. Journal of Occupational and Organizational Psychology. 2010;**83**(3):579-599

[43] Brown SP, Leigh TW. A new look at psychological climate and its relationship to job involvement, effort, and performance. Journal of Applied Psychology. 1996;**81**(4):358-368

[44] Lee J, Ok C. Drivers of work engagement: An examination of core self-evaluations and psychological climate among hotel employees. International Journal of Hospitality Management. 2015;**44**:84-98. DOI: 10.1016/j.ijhm.2014.10.008

[45] Kroth M, Keeler C. Caring as a managerial strategy. Human Resource Development Review. 2009;**8**(4):506-531. DOI: 10.1177/1534484309341558

[46] Barnes DC, Collier JE. Investigating work engagement in the service environment. 2010

[47] Biddison EL, Paine L, Murakami P, Herzke C, Weaver SJ. Associations between safety culture and employee engagement over time: A retrospective analysis. BMJ Quality and Safety. 2015:1-7

[48] Huhtala M, Tolvanen A, Mauno S, Feldt T. The associations between ethical organizational culture, burnout, and engagement: A multilevel study. Journal of Business and Psychology. 2015;**30**(2):399-414

[49] Dirani KM. Measuring the learning organization culture, organizational commitment and job satisfaction in the Lebanese banking sector. Human Resource Development International. 2009;**12**(2):189-208

[50] Islam T, Khan MM, Bukhari FH. The role of organizational learning culture and psychological empowerment in reducing turnover intention and enhancing citizenship behavior. The Learning Organization. 2016;**23**(2/3):156-169

[51] Mitonga-Monga J, Flotman AP, Cilliers F. Workplace ethics culture and work engagement: The mediating effect of ethical leadership in a developing world context. Journal of Psychology in Africa. 2016;**26**(4):326-333

[52] Lee MCC, Idris MA, Delfabbro PH. The linkages between hierarchical culture and empowering leadership and their effects on employees' work engagement: Work meaningfulness as a mediator. International Journal of Stress Management. 2017;**24**(4):392-415

[53] Collier S, Fitzpatrick J, Siedlecki SL, Dolansky MA. Employee engagement and a culture of safety in the intensive care unit. Journal of Nursing Administration. 2016;**46**(1):49-54

[54] Abbasi E, Zamani-Miandashti N. The role of transformational leadership, organizational culture and organizational learning in improving the performance of Iranian agricultural faculties. Higher Education. 2013;**66**(4):505-519

[55] Claeys M, Deplaecie M, Vanderplancke T, Delbaere I, Myny D, Beeckman D, et al. The difference in learning culture and learning performance between a traditional clinical placement, a dedicated education unit and work-based learning. Nurse Education Today. 2015;**35**(9):70-77

[56] Hahn MH, Lee KC, Lee DS. Network structure, organizational learning

culture, and employee creativity in system integration companies: The mediating effects of exploitation and exploration. Computers in Human Behavior. 2015;**42**:167-175

[57] Cooper AL, Huscroft JR, Overstreet RE, Hazen BT. Knowledge management for logistics service provider: The role of learning culture. Industrial Management & Data Systems. 2016;**116**(3)

[58] Becker GS. Human Capital: A Theoretical and Empirical Analysis, with Special Reference to Education. Vol. 2. National Bureau of Economic Research; 1975

[59] Javed B, Bashir S, Rawwas M, Arjoon S. Islamic work ethic, innovative work behaviour, and adaptive performance: The mediating mechanism and an interacting effect. Current Issues in Tourism. 2017;**20**(6):647-663

[60] Banerjee P, Gupta R, Bates R. Influence of organizational learning culture on knowledge worker's motivation to transfer training: Testing moderating effects of learning transfer climate. Current Psychology. 2016

Chapter 9

Effects of Information Technologies on Organizational Culture: A Discussion Based on the Key Role of Organizational Structure

Eser Erdurmazlı

Abstract

This chapter discusses the influences of information technologies on cultural features of organizations with an emphasis on the concept of "organizational structure" because research shows that organizational culture and organizational structure are in a very close relationship. In this regard, it argues that information technologies can have direct and indirect effects on organizational cultures based on the information technologies' influences on organizational structures and the processes, activities, and human relations within these structures. Underlining different and controversial approaches and findings in the literature, this study makes some deductions by referring to important features of information technologies and organizational culture. Therefore, the approaches and evaluations given here are thought to be useful for the practitioners and students who are interested in the subject and the academic staff who are interested in doing research on this subject.

Keywords: organizational culture, organizational structure, information technologies, information, knowledge

1. Introduction

Today, information has become the main component of what we produce, do, buy, and consume. Having an economic value in almost all products and services that meet the needs of today's societies, it has been now obligatory for individuals and organizations to obtain information technologies and to actively use them in both work and social life domains. Hence, in the current information age, where information is seen as power, this situation has made it imperative for organizations to become increasingly information-based and to benefit from information technologies in many processes and activities.

The intensive use of information technologies in many functions and processes has also required some changes in organizations [1]. This is due to the fact that information technologies, unlike traditional technologies, do not only change the technical fields but also affect the communication channels, decision-making functions and mechanisms, control, etc. [2]. Consequently, one of the most striking developments is on organizational structures that are becoming increasingly flattened and horizontal. Relatedly, information technologies have begun to take over the role of middle management, which supports decision-making processes of senior management and has reduced the importance of this level [3–5]. Similarly, while information technologies enable managers to obtain faster, more accurate, and more information [6–8], it also provides lower-level managers with more information about the general situation of the organization, the nature of current problems, and important organizational matters [9–12].

Moreover, information technologies also have an important potential in determining whether organizations have a mechanical or an organic structure [13]. Within the mechanical organizational structures, people do not have much autonomy, and behaviors expected from employees are being careful and obedience to upper authority and respect for traditions. In such organizations, predictability, consistency, and stability are desirable phenomena. In contrast, people in organic structures have more freedom in shaping and controlling their activities, and being enthusiastic, creative, and taking risks have important places among the desired behaviors [14].

Accordingly, information technologies begin to influence the cultural values of the organization over time, through these transformations they create on organizational structures, processes, and operations. In other words, the fact that organizational structures are mechanical or organic causes the formation of diverse cultural values in organizations [15]. Therefore, the desired cultural values in mechanical organizations are quite different from those in organic structures [1, 16, 17]. In this context, *this chapter deals with the influences of information technologies on cultural characteristics of organizations along with the reflections of the use of these technologies on organizational structures and their functioning*.

When we look at studies on the relations between organizational culture and information technologies, we generally see the studies on the effects of culture on technology adaptation or use [18–21], as well as on the effects of certain specific information technologies and applications (e.g., e-mail use, group support practices, etc.) on some aspects of any organizational culture [22–31]. However, the number of studies that consider the use of information technologies as a "whole" and that address "why" and "how" its effects on organizational culture occurred is still limited. And so, *this chapter aims* to examine and discuss the overall effects of the usage and intensity of information technologies established in organizations on the cultural life within.

In this context, the chapter plan is as follows: *Firstly*, the basic concepts related to information and information technologies are included. Emphasis is placed on the meaning differences between knowledge and information, and their connections to information technologies are tried to be explained briefly. *Secondly*, the effects of information technologies on organizational structure are given particular attention. The reason for this is that as a system of values, beliefs, assumptions, and practices [32], organizational culture encompasses many features closely related to structures of organizations. *Thirdly*, possible links between organizational structure and organizational culture are included. *Fourthly*, important theoretical approaches and studies on the relationships between information technologies and organizational culture are provided. *Finally*, by deepening a bit more and by emphasizing key points, some important arguments are discussed.

2. Information and information technologies

In the literature, the concepts of information and knowledge are sometimes expressed by a single term, "information." However, although the concepts of knowledge and information are intertwined, they are two different concepts that have different meanings and describe different phenomena. The reason for this is that knowledge is also included in the concept of information as it is transformed into a commodity when it begins to be processed, stored, and shared by information technologies.

Becoming the basic elements of today's economic, social, and cultural systems, information is obtained in a certain hierarchy. The images are at the beginning of the process, and the process is completed with a hierarchical staging in the form of data, information, and knowledge, respectively [33]. *Image* is located in the first step of the process. Humans copy the picture of any object and event they previously perceived by sensory organs. When faced with a similar phenomenon in the later stages of life, these pictures in the mind are redesigned. We call these pictures of realities occurring in the human mind as images [33]. The next stage, the *data*, contains symbols that represent events and their properties. For this reason, data are expressed as figures and/or facts without content and interpretation [34]. *Information* that constitutes the next stage of the process and is mixed with knowledge and used interchangeably is expressed as a reporting of one system's own status to another system [33]. In information, associated data are combined for a specific purpose. Therefore, we can explain information as meaningful data [35]. *Knowledge*, on the other hand, is defined as personalized information that allows people to fully and accurately grasp what is happening around them and manifests itself in the form of thoughts, insights, intuition, ideas, lessons learned, practices, and experiences [36]. According to Kautz and Thaysen [37] who stated that knowledge is found only in the people's minds, knowledge is, therefore, a subjective formation. In other words, knowledge is the form of information enriched with interpretation, analysis, and context [38]. However, here, it should be emphasized again by highlighting a very important issue that *knowledge is also accepted as information when this knowledge begins to be processed, stored, shared, and used over information technologies.* Therefore, after this, when talking about information, one should consider not only the information created by the data brought together in a meaningful way but also the knowledge shared and used over information technologies.

On the other hand, *information technologies*, used as the most important tool of generating value today, are defined as the technologies that enable processes such as recording and storing data, producing information through certain operational processes, and accessing, storing, and transmitting this produced information effectively and efficiently [39–46]. The term information technologies is used to cover computer and electronic communication technologies, as they are now inseparably intertwined in literature and everyday use and are generally used in this way [47]. In this context, data processing systems, management information systems (MIS), office automation systems, executive support systems, expert systems, intranet and extranet, electronic mail (e-mail), group applications (groupware), database management systems, decision support systems, artificial intelligence, and telecommunication systems can be given as examples of information technologies [33, 48, 49].

3. Information technologies and organizational structure

Towards the end of the twentieth century, the rapid changes with the impact of developments in information technologies led to the emergence of customer satisfaction-based, learning, knowledge-based, and constantly changing organizations [50]. The fact that organizations have become considerably information-based and benefit from information technologies intensively in their activities and processes has made also the changes in their organizational structures mandatory [1]. Accordingly, the effects of information technologies on organizational structure will be summarized under the subtitles of differentiation, centralization, and standardization/formalization, which are the three main components of organizational structure [15].

3.1 Effects of information technologies on differentiation

Differentiation within an organization occurs in three ways: Specialization/division of labor, horizontal and vertical differentiation, and hierarchy and size [15]. Specialization refers to the amount of different expertise or types of work [51, 52]. Specialization generally increases the number of subunits and makes it harder to understand the larger structure that people contribute to with their skills and expertise [53]. Information technologies have the potential to reduce this tendency by providing more access to information and experts at this point. In this way, access to information resources provides synergy [54].

Vertical and horizontal differentiation refers to the amount of hierarchical levels in an organization [55]. Information technologies, with the support of problem solving and decision-making, lead to the emergence of more flattened organizational structures as they require fewer levels within the hierarchy [56]. Since information technologies give employees in lower positions more autonomy to harmonize their activities, this can allow them to find and try better methods while performing their work. In this context, we can increasingly see that organizational structures have become horizontal and strengthened and that virtual organizations have begun to emerge as the most cost-effective structure [17].

In terms of hierarchy and size, Heinze and Stuart [4] argue that the mid-level management staff is unnecessary, increases bureaucracy, reduces efficiency, and has no function in organizations any more. Since most of the tasks performed by mid-level executives can be fulfilled by computers, both less costly and faster, information technology has begun to take over the role of mid-level management, which supports the decision-making process of senior management [5]. Sharing the same opinion, Fulk and DeSanctis [57] also stated that the largely witnessed situation in modern organizational designs is the reduction of intermediate-level managers and administrative support.

3.2 Effects of information technologies on centralization

Centralization points to the extent to which decision-making power within an organization is scattered or centered [58]. Due to increasing local and global competition, many companies have started to leave their strategic decision-making task further down the organization to benefit from the expert people with more precise and timely local knowledge [10]. Information technologies affect these efforts directly in two ways. Firstly, information technologies increase local knowledge by contributing to obtaining closer information about market trends, opportunities, and customers. Secondly, information technologies can create synergies for organizations because, thanks to information technologies, communication and coordination between distributed decision makers, central planners, and senior managers can be realized more effectively and efficiently [59].

However, whether information technologies will lead to centralization or decentralization is a very controversial question. Regarding centralization, it enables managers to acquire faster, more accurate, and more information, reduces uncertainty, and allows them to make decisions that they cannot make before [6–8]. Conversely, by the use of other forms of information technologies (e.g., electronic bulletin boards), decentralization provides more information to lower- and mid-level managers about the general situation of the organization and the nature of current matters and problems [9–12]. Raymond et al. [60] argued that because information technologies facilitate the use and transmission of information by all levels and units in the organization, it enables top management, which is the decision authority, to be disabled in certain areas and the decentralization of control. Thach and Woodman [61] maintained that this is due to the fact that as a result of sharing information at lower levels with the help of information technologies, this power of senior management has decreased to a certain extent, and the knowledge and participation of the staff in organizational matters have increased.

The literature shows that information technologies allow both centralization and decentralization. Researchers are in the agreement that information technologies make it possible for organizational managers to leave their decision-making power to a large part of the hierarchical levels without compromising the quality and timeliness of the decision [62, 63]. Keen [64] combined the concepts of centralization and decentralization and used the term "federated organization" in which organizations do not have to choose either because information technologies simultaneously allow centralization-decentralization [64, 65].

3.3 Effects of information technologies on standardization/formalization

Formalization is the process of detailing how activities are coordinated for organizational purposes in order for employees and organizational units to respond routinely to recurring situations [51, 66]. Formalization involves rules, instructions, shared values, and norms [67]. In fact, formalization is based on the objective of more efficiency and less uncertainty [13].

Information technologies provide the ability to reduce the negative effects of formalization by facilitating the documenting and retrieving of information on organizational occurrences and endeavors that make behaviors and processes more consistent through formalization [63]. The more information technologies assist in reducing search times and preventing downtime, the more the administrative cost of formalization decreases and the productivity increases, which ultimately benefits the path to innovation [68].

4. Organizational structure and organization culture

Different organizational structures lead to the development of different cultural values [15]. The fact that the structure which an organization has established to control its activities and is defined as a formal system consisting of duties and authority relations is mechanical or organic causes the emergence of completely different cultural values, rules, and norms [69]. While mechanical structures are vertical, highly centralized, and almost everything in them are standardized, organic structures are horizontal, decentralized, and based on mutual adaptation [14]. People feel relatively less autonomous in vertical and centralized organizations, and being careful, obeying the upper authority, and respecting traditions are among the desired behaviors. Therefore, in a mechanical organizational structure, there are cultural values where predictability and stability are important [69]. In contrast, in horizontal and decentralized organizations, people can freely choose their own activities and control them. Creativity, courage, and risk-taking are given importance as desired behaviors. Therefore, organic structures contribute to the formation of cultures that value innovation and flexibility [15].

Organizational structure is also important for the development of cultural values that support integration and coordination. In a structure with stable task and role relations, sharing of rules and norms is more since there will be no communication problems and the information flow will be fast [70]. In organizations where the sharing of cultural values, norms, and rules is at a high level, the level of performance also increases [15]. Particularly in team or matrix structures where face-to-face communication is intense, the sharing of these cultural values and common reactions to the problems develop more rapidly [9].

Whether an organization is centralized or not causes different cultural values to emerge. In decentralized structures, authority is divided into subordinate levels, and an environment is created for the formation of cultural values in which creativity and innovation are rewarded [13]. Employees are allowed to use the organization's resources and work in projects that they want, by spending some of their time in these projects, thus contributing to the production of innovative and creative products and services [15]. The structures of such organizations constitute the cultural values that give their employees the message "as long as it is in the interest of the organization, it is okay to do things in an innovative and the way you want."

Conversely, in some organizations, it may be more important for employees not to decide on their own and all activities to be followed and controlled by their superiors. In such cases, a centralized structure is preferred to create cultural values that will ensure accountability and obedience [71]. Through norms and rules, all employees are expected to behave honestly and consistently and inform their superiors about wrongs or mistakes, because this is the only acceptable form of behavior within these structures [72].

5. Information technologies and organization culture

Since working on the factors that determine the consequences of the adoption and use of information technologies, researchers have focused on people's beliefs, values, assumptions, and codes of conduct. As a result, they have given names to this research field such as "socio-technical systems," "social system," "social structure," and most recently "culture" [73]. For example, Markus and Robey [23] using "social elements" and Barley [26] using "social system" or "social structure" tried to explain this phenomenon. When examined more closely, it is seen that the details that these authors emphasize while depicting the case are the assumptions, beliefs, and values that exist in common among the group members, and this corresponds to the definition of organizational culture.

Research examining the relationships between information technologies and values, beliefs, and norms belonging to a particular group has gone through certain stages and used rich and complex research models to explain the relationships in each of these stages [74]. In the first studies on information technology applications, it has been suggested that information technologies cause changes in various organizational phenomena including structural features and thus have certain effects on organizations [74]. For instance, in some studies on adoption of groupware software, several researchers have used this deterministic approach to describe how groupware use affects communication and collaboration among employees and their productivity [27, 28]. These studies assume that certain results will certainly emerge after the adoption of information technologies, without considering the motives or activities that shape the use of information technologies by managers and employees. Like much more deterministic studies, these authors often assumed that information technologies would have predetermined influences on the adoption of information technologies, regardless of the environment in which information technologies were applied, how they were applied, and the users' specific behaviors and particular purposes.

The second group of views concerning the relationships between organizational culture and information technologies includes the fact that information technologies are seen as a tool that can be used for any change that managers desire to make in organizational practices [22]. In studies in this approach, researchers believe that there is a wide range of possibilities to identify changes in organizational culture, structure, processes, and performance [22, 75]. Researchers from this tradition presume that with the right choice of information technologies and appropriate system design, managers can achieve whatever goals they desire.

These works were mostly adopted in the 1980s and reflect a perspective that managers think can manipulate organizational culture in the way they want. Often called "management and control," "a functional or instrumental approach" to organizational culture, this methodology has caused serious debate in the literature [76]. This approach attributes great powers to the management level in this regard, which conflicts with anthropologists' views that culture cannot be consciously controlled and goes much deeper to understand it [76]. Robey and Azevido [77] also do not accept the rational thought on the assumption that culture can be manipulated directly in this way.

Studies with this rational perspective in the information technology literature assume that managers can use information technologies as a leverage to make changes in the norms of behavior, strategy, structure, and performance among members within the organization. For example, in studies on group support systems (GSS), we find managers' beliefs that they can use collaborative technologies to create a more cooperative organizational culture. This perspective was not accepted by Karsten [78] and some experimental research on GSS [30, 79]. Organizational necessity is no longer accepted, as it is viewed by information technology researchers as an overly simple approach [23, 80].

Researchers who take another approach suggest that information technologies and organizational culture can interact with each other to produce various results [22, 23]. These results can be in the form of adoption and effective use of information technologies (if there is a harmony between organizational culture and information technologies) or user reluctance, refusal, or sabotage (if no fit). Researchers who have been working on information systems since the 1980s have focused on understanding information technology features and functionality that cause effective or problematic information technology applications and the interaction between users' values, assumptions, and other elements of organizational culture. In this regard, Romm et al. [81] argued that many forms of information technologies comprise cultural assumptions embedded within themselves and these assumptions may conflict with existing values of a particular organization. The authors argued that these embedded assumptions present information technologies as a "cultural boundary" and that a cultural analysis should be made to predict compliance or incompatibility. The authors in this approach warn managers to think of organizational culture as a binding limitation in information technology applications. In a warning by Pliskin et al. [76], managers are advised not to try to change the culture of the organization. Regarding this issue, Orlikowski [30] cites Lotus Notes (a group software) application at Alpha Corporation, a consultancy company. In this example, this system, which was established by the CEO of the company only with the benefits to be obtained, did not create the expected effects, became unsuccessful, and disappointed due to reasons such as no cultural analysis and inadequate training. Employees responded to the use of Notes with resistance and refrained from using it. The reason for this was that the employees in this organization, which had a competitive culture where information was seen as a power, avoided sharing information with others. As a result, this incompatibility between the collaborative culture that Notes had in itself and the competitive culture of the organization in question had failed this application of information technologies.

In a different approach, it is stated that information technologies and culture are not fixed and they are more flexible in terms of change [23, 75]. Managers in this approach may set specific goals for the use of information technologies, but actual results of the use of information technologies are not deterministic, and results cannot be predicted or controlled even under the best conditions [23]. The effects of information technologies are not deterministic because technology has interpretable flexibility considering that it can have different meanings for different employees. Similar technology can be interpreted in a different way by distinct people, based on certain assumptions, beliefs, and values. Robey and coauthors [24, 25], for instance, showed that it would be an empty attempt for organizational managers to try to intentionally manipulate the effects of these technologies, since there are many ways that diverse employees can configure a particular technology in different social environments.

Gopal and Prasad [31] also achieved similar results in their work on group support system (GSS), claiming that for researchers seeking fixed laws or regulations on how information technologies affect user behaviors, this would be an impossible goal to pursue. Conversely, the results of using information technologies depend on the symbolic meanings that information technologies have for a particular user. This work of Gopal and Prasad [31] expresses similar results with the work of Barley [26] and Robey and Sahay [25]. The authors stated that the symbolic meanings of certain technologies for users affect their perceptions of information technologies and their specific behaviors.

6. Discussions

In the light of the above-mentioned approaches, arguments, and important studies in the literature, it will be useful to discuss some important points by deepening a little more and by emphasizing the key features related to the concepts of information, information technologies, and organizational culture.

First, organizational culture is a complex phenomenon that develops and changes in a historical process [32, 82, 83]. Thus, although it might seem like a plain and simple concept, organizational culture includes many subdimensions and processes. When considered as a complex pattern of these interactions of many factors with each other, it is also a difficult process to identify the direct and indirect effects of information technologies on organizational culture within this cluster of relationships and interactions. Moreover, culture is not a phenomenon that changes and develops in a short time and is therefore open to manipulations of managers. On the contrary, from this point of view, it is not possible to easily achieve control over cultural changes, and it is necessary to go much deeper [76]. So, it is not rational to expect that the rapid developments and changes in information technologies will cause changes in cultural characteristics at the same speed. In this sense, it could be inaccurate to seek direct relationships between two phenomena in question, whose rates of change are quite different.

Second, for cultural changes, there must also be changes in the basic assumptions, beliefs, and values on which the culture is built [84]. It would be misleading to expect little or intensive use of information technologies to cause changes in these rooted assumptions. For the desired changes in these basic assumptions, beliefs, and values, it is necessary to design the structure accordingly, to recruit employees who are qualified for the targeted culture, and to set ethical values and property rights to employees in accordance with this culture [15]. In this sense, information technologies may only catalyze the contribution of organizational structure to organizational culture.

Third, there are many and different types of hardware and software that fall under the scope of information technologies. It is not logical to accept all of them as homogeneous technologies in all aspects (with the same functions and features, similar usage areas, standard conditions they are applied, similar intentions, and behaviors of all users), and it can be, therefore, misleading to carry out research under a single "IT" concept from this perspective. The reason for this is that, as stated in the sections above, cultural features of each information technology application or product embedded in it might be different. The interactions between the cultural characteristics of the environment in which information technologies are applied and the unique cultural contents of information technologies may cause different results on the culture of the organization.

Fourth, contrary to what is believed, some of cultural features that we anticipate to support information technology applications and products may be interpreted otherwise by diverse people contingent on different assumptions, beliefs, and values. In fact, Robey et al. [24, 25] showed that managers cannot control the effects of these technologies, since different users can configure a particular technology in numerous ways in different social environments. Also, Gopal and Prasad [31] argued that this would be an impossible achievement for researchers looking for fixed laws or regulations on how information technologies affect user behaviors.

Fifth, information technologies were defined above as technologies that enable processing, storage, and sharing of information. The key concept in this definition is "knowledge-based" information and not the technology itself. Therefore, what makes information technologies essential and important is the information itself. According to the definition of knowledge, the most significant characteristic that differentiates it from information is its being a product of the human mind [37]. Because knowledge is the interpretation of information and expresses the value produced from it, qualifying information technologies as good-bad, useful-useless, and necessary-unnecessary can be a meaningless evaluation. So, the basic thing that creates value-added for organizations is not the technology used but the information itself, which is processed, stored, and shared on this technology. In this context, even if it is the latest, most advanced, and most expensive technology in the world, if the organization does not have a qualified human resource capable of producing knowledge that will create value-added, an appropriate organizational structure and culture that will activate this creative potential, and a management approach, all investments in these technologies will also be wasted.

7. Conclusions

This chapter has aimed to examine the impacts of information technologies on organizations' cultures, and for this purpose, a special emphasis is given to the concept of "organizational structure" within the theoretical framework presented above. The most important reason for this is that relevant literature shows that organizational culture and organizational structure are in a very close relationship. Indeed, when the question items in the Denison organizational culture scale [85], which is the most frequently used in the literature, are examined, it is possible to see that most of these items point to many features of organizational structure concerning centralization, formalization, and differentiation dimensions. Therefore, it is a very rational approach to expect that information technologies can have direct and indirect effects on organizational cultures based on the influences of information technologies on structures of organizations. However, it should be underlined that different and controversial approaches and findings in the literature mentioned above on the relations between information technologies and organizational culture generate question marks in the minds as well.

In this regard, it is already quite difficult to draw a clear picture of the impacts of information technologies on cultural characteristics of organizations. The number of studies on the subject in the literature is still very limited. Accordingly, it is necessary to underline the great need for interdisciplinary studies in this field. But still, this study argues that the main factor that determines the actual impact and value of information technologies, which have become an integral part of human life in today's world, is the information itself rather than technology, and it should be kept in mind that information technologies can only function as a means or tool in this knowledge-based social, economic, and cultural life. In other words, the determinant of the benefits, meaning, and importance of information technologies might be the conditions created by organizational factors such as cultural environment and organizational structure where knowledge is created, developed, and used and human resources have become the most important capital element and source of wealth.

Conflict of interest

The author declares no conflict of interest.

Author details

Eser Erdurmazlı
Gendarmerie and Coast Guard Academy, Ankara, Turkey

*Address all correspondence to: akadem06@yahoo.com

References

[1] Drucker PF. Knowledge worker productivity: The biggest challenge. California Management Review. 1999;**41**(2):79-94

[2] Bloodgood JM, Morrow JL Jr. Strategic organizational change: Exploring the roles of environmental structure, internal conscious awareness and knowledge. Journal of Management Studies. 2003;**40**(7):1761-1782

[3] Rockart J, DeLong D. Executive Support Systems: The Emergence of Top Management Computer Use. Burr Ridge, IL: Dow-Jones-Irwin; 1988

[4] Heintze T, Stuart B. Information technology and restructuring in public organizations: Does adoption of information technology affect organizational structures, communications and decision making? Journal of Public Administration Research and Theory. 2000;**10**(4):778-812

[5] Littler CR, Wiesner R, Dunford R. The dynamics of delayering: Changing management structures in three countries. Journal of Management Studies. 2003;**40**(3):225-227

[6] Blau PM, Falbe CM, McKinley W, Tracey PK. Technology and organization in manufacturing. Administrative Science Quarterly. 1976;**21**:20-40

[7] Child J, Partridge B. Lost Managers Supervisors in Industry and Society. Cambridge MA: Cambridge University Press; 1982

[8] Lado AA, Zhang MJ. Expert systems, knowledge development and utilization and sustained competitive advantage: A resource-based model. Journal of Management. 1998;**24**(4):489-509

[9] Argyres NS. The impact of information technology on coordination: Evidence from the B2 stealth bomber. Organization Science. 1999;**10**(2):162-180

[10] Fulk J, Dutton W. Videoconferencing as an organizational information system: Assessing the role of electronic meetings. Systems, Objectives and Solutions. 1984;**4**:105-118

[11] Lawler EE. Substitute for hierarchy. Organizational Dynamics. 1998;**17**:477-491

[12] Zenger T, Hesterly W. Desegregation of corporations: Selective intervention, high-powered incentives and modular units. Organization Science. 1997;**8**:209-222

[13] Perrow C. Normal Accidents. NY: Basic Books; 1984

[14] Ülgen H, Mirze SK. İşletmelerde stratejik yönetim. No: 113. İstanbul: Literatür Yayınları; 2006

[15] Jones GR. Organizational Theory, Design, and Change. 5th ed. Upper Saddle River: Prentice Hall; 2007

[16] Cusumano MA, Selby RW. Microsoft's Secrets. New York: The Free Press; 1995

[17] Shao YP, Liao SY, Wang HQ. A model of virtual organizations. The Academy of Management Executive. 1988;**12**(4):305-312

[18] Peters TJ, Waterman RH. In Search of Excellence. New York: Harper and Row; 1982

[19] Meyerson D, Martin J. Cultural change: An integration of three different views. Journal of Management Studies. 1987;**24**(6):623-647

[20] Alvesson M. Understanding Organizational Culture. London: Sage Publications; 2002

[21] Schwarz H, Davis S. Matching corporate culture and business strategy. Organizational Dynamics. 1981;**10**:30-48

[22] Markus ML, Robey D. The organizational validity of MIS. Human Relations. 1983;**36**:203-226

[23] Markus ML, Robey D. Information technology and organizational change: Causal structure in theory and research. Management Science. 1988;**34**:583-598

[24] Robey D, Boudreau MC. Accounting for the contradictory organizational consequences of IT. Information Systems Research. 1999:**10**(2);167-185

[25] Robey D, Sahay S. Transforming work through IT: A comparative study of geographic IS in country government. Information Systems Research. 1996;**7**(1):93-110

[26] Barley SR. Technology as an occasion for structuring: Evidence from observations of CT scanners and the social order of radiology departments. Administrative Science Quarterly. 1986;**31**:78-108

[27] King WR. Strategic issues in groupware. Information Systems Management. 1996;**13**(2):73-75

[28] Clark AS, Downing CE, Coleman D. Groupware at big six consulting firms: How successful was it? In: Coleman D, editor. Groupware: Collaborative Strategies for Corporate LANs and Intranets. Upper Saddle River, NJ: Prentice-Hall; 1997

[29] Zack MH. McKenney J.L. social context and interaction in ongoing computer-supported management groups. Organization Science. 1995;**6**(4):394-422

[30] Orlikowski W. Learning from notes: Organizational issues in groupware implementation. The Information Society. 1993;**9**(3):237-250

[31] Gopal A, Prasad P. Understanding GDSS in symbolic context: Shifting the focus from technology to interaction. Management Information Systems Quarterly. 2000;**24**(3):509-546

[32] Schein EH. Organizational Culture and Leadership. London: Josey-Bass; 1986

[33] Tutar H. Yönetim bilgi sistemi. İstanbul: Seçkin Yayıncılık 1. Baskı; 2006

[34] Kalseth K, Cummings S. Knowledge management: Development strategy or business strategy? Information Development. 2001;**17**(3):163-172

[35] Dervişoğlu HG. Stratejik bilgi yönetimi. İstanbul: Dışbank; 2004

[36] Barutçugil İ. Bilgi yönetimi. İstanbul: Kariyer Yayıncılık; 2002

[37] Kautz K, Kim T. Knowledge, learning and IT support in a small software company. Journal of Knowledge Management. 2001;**5**(4):349-357

[38] Duffy J. Knowledge management: To be or not to be. The Information Management Journal. 2000;**34**:64-67

[39] Andolsen AA. Managing digital information: The emerging technologies. Records Management Quarterly. 1999;**33**(2):8-15

[40] Campbell R. Share the knowledge. Molding Systems. 1999;**57**(10):14-18

[41] Edwards M. Enablers for IP videoconferencing. Communication News. 1999;**36**(12):90-99

[42] Grahm JR. Eleven ways the internet is playing havoc with business. Lunra's Marketfacts. 1999;**18**(6):11-13

[43] Schober D. The telephony freeway. Telephony. 1999;**237**(2):14-14

[44] Spiegelman LL. CRM solution unlocks database goldmine. Computer Reseller News. 1999;November:5-6

[45] Tarabour RM. Building standards-based unified messaging systems. Computer Technology Review. 1999;**19**(5):27-56

[46] Wildstrom SH. The palm is mightier. Business Week. November (3655); 1999

[47] Bensghir TK. Bilgi teknolojileri ve örgütsel değişim. Ankara: TODAİE Yayınları; 1996

[48] Laudon CK, Laudon PJ. Management Information Systems. 8th ed. Upper Saddle River, New Jersey: Pearson Prentice Hall; 2004

[49] Elibol H. Bilişim teknolojileri kullanımının işletmelerin organizasyon yapıları üzerindeki etkileri. Selçuk Üniversitesi Sosyal Bilimler Enstitüsü Dergisi. 2005;**13**:155-162

[50] Alavi M, Leidner DE. Knowledge management and knowledge management systems: Conceptual foundations and research issues. MIS Quarterly. 2001;**25**(1):107-136

[51] Aiken M, Bacharach SB, French LL. Organizational structure, work process, and proposal making in administrative bureaucracies. Academy of Management Journal. 1980;**23**(4):631-652

[52] Hage J, Aiken M. Program change and organizational properties: A comparative analysis. Journal of Sociology. 1967;**72**(5):503-519

[53] Lawrence PR, Lorsch JW. Organization and Environment. Boston, MA: Harvard Business School, Division of Research; 1967

[54] Ciborra C, Lanzara GG. Designing dynamic artifacts computer systems as formative contexts. In: Gahardi P, editor. Symbols and Artifacts. Berlin: De Gruyter; 1990

[55] Damanpour F. Organizational innovation: A meta-analysis of effects of determinants and moderators. Academy of Management Review. 1991;**34**(3):555-590

[56] Snow CC, Lipnack J, Stamps J. The virtual organization: Promises and payoffs, large and small. In: Cooper CL, Rousseau DM, editors. The Virtual Organization. Chichester: Wiley; 1999

[57] Fulk J, DeSanctis G. Electronic communication and changing organizational forms. Organization Science. 1995;**6**(4):337-349

[58] Pfeffer J. Power in Organizations. Boston: Pitman; 1981

[59] Tushman ML, Anderson PC, O'Reilley C. In: Tushman ML, Anderson PC, editors. Technology Cycles, Innovation Streams and Ambidextrous Organizations: Organization Renewal through Innovation and Strategic Change, Managing Strategic Innovation and Change—A Collection of Readings. New York: Oxford University Press; 1997

[60] Raymond M, Pare G, Bergeron F. Matching information technology and organizational structure: An empirical study with implications for performance. European Journal of Information Systems. 1995;**4**(2):3-16

[61] Thach L, Woodman RW. Organizational change and information technology: Managing on the edge of cyberspace. Organizational Dynamics. 1994;**23**(1):42-58

[62] Groth L. Future Organizational Design. New York: John Wiley and Sons; 1999

[63] Huber GP. A theory of the effects of advanced information technologies on organizational design, intelligence and decision making. Academy of Management Review. 1990;**15**(1):47-71

[64] Keen PGW. Telecommunications and organizational choice. In: Fulk J, Steinfield C, editors. Organizations and Communication Technology. Newbury Park: Sage; 1990

[65] Burris BH. Technocracy at Work. New York: State University of New York Press; 1993

[66] Blau JR, McKinley W. Ideal complexity and innovation. Administrative Science Quarterly. 1979;**24**(2):200-219

[67] Weber M. The Theory of Social and Economic Organization. New York: Oxford University Press; 1947

[68] Daft RL, Becker W. The Innovative Organization. New York, Elsevier; 1978

[69] Hatch MJ. The dynamics of organizational culture. Academy of Management Review. 1993;**18**(4):657-693

[70] Dolan SL, Garcia S. Managing by values: Cultural redesign for strategic organizational change at the dawn of the twenty-first century. The Journal of Management Development. 2002;**21**(2):101-117

[71] İzci F, Arslan NT. Bilgi toplumuna geçiş sürecinde örgütsel yapıda meydana gelen değişimler: Bilişim teknolojisi örgütsel yapı ilişkisi. İÜ Siyasal Bilgiler Fakültesi Dergisi. 2004;**30**(March):31-50

[72] Mintzberg H. The Structuring of Organizational Cultures. Upper Saddle River: Prentice Hall; 1979

[73] Bostrom RP, Heinen JS. MIS problems and failures: A sociotechnical perspective. MIS Quarterly. 1977;**1**(13):17-32

[74] Gallivan M, Strite M. Information technology and culture: Identifying fragmentary and holistic perspectives of culture. Information and Organization. 2005;**15**(4):295-338

[75] Orlikowski W. The duality of technology: Rethinking the concept of technology in organizations. Organization Science. 1992;**3**(3):398-427

[76] Pliskin N, Romm C, Lee AS, Weber Y. Presumed v. actual organizational culture: Managerial implications for implementation of information systems. The Computer Journal. 1993;**36**(2):141-152

[77] Robey D, Azevedo A. Cultural analysis of the organizational consequences of IT. Accounting, Management and Information Technology. 1994;**4**(1):23-37

[78] Karsten H. Collaboration and collaborative information technologies: A review of the evidence. Data Base for Advances in Information Systems. 1999;**30**(2):231-257

[79] Vandenbosch B, Ginzberg MJ. Lotus notes and collaboration: Plus ca change. Journal of MIS. 1996/1997;**13**(3):65-82

[80] Ciborra C. From Control to Drift: The Dynamics of Corporate Information Infrastructures. Oxford: Oxford University Press; 2000

[81] Romm T, Pliskin N, Weber Y, Lee AS. Identifying organizational culture clash in MIS implementation: When is it worth the effort. Information & Management. 1991;**21**(2):99-109

[82] Hofstede G. Cultures and Organizations-Software of the Mind. London: McGraw Hill İnternational; 1994

[83] Şişman M. Örgüt kültürü, No:732. Eskişehir: Anadolu Üniversitesi Yayınları; 1994

[84] Schein EH. Organizational Culture and Leadership. San Francisco: Josey-Bass Inc. Publishers; 1992

[85] Denison DR, Neale W. Denison organizational culture survey. Ann Arbor, MI: Denison Consulting; 2000